JUDGES:
LEADERS IN CRISIS TIMES

JUDGES:
LEADERS IN CRISIS TIMES
DONALD K. CAMPBELL

While this book is intended for the reader's personal enjoyment and profit, it is also intended for group study. A Leader's Guide with Reproducible Response Sheets is available from your local bookstore or from the publisher.

VICTOR BOOKS®

A DIVISION OF SCRIPTURE PRESS PUBLICATIONS INC.
USA CANADA ENGLAND

Unless otherwise noted, Scripture quotations in this book are from the *New American Standard Bible,* © the Lockman Foundation 1960, 1962, 1963, 1968, 1971, 1972, 1973, 1975, 1977. Quotations marked NIV are from the *Holy Bible, New International Version,* © 1973, 1978, 1984, International Bible Society. Used by permission of Zondervan Bible Publishers. Quotations marked RSV are from the *Revised Standard Version of the Bible,* © 1946, 1952, 1971, 1973. Quotations marked KJV are taken from the *Authorized (King James) Version.*

Recommended Dewey Decimal Classification: 222.3

Suggested Subject Heading: BIBLE, OLD TESTAMENT—HISTORY: GEOGRAPHY: BIBLICAL CHARACTERS

Library of Congress Catalog Card Number: 89-60172

ISBN: 0-89693-741-0

CONTENTS

DEDICATION

"Grandchildren are the crown of old men"
(Proverbs 17:6).
With a grandfather's love and prayers, I dedicate this
work to Jason, Heather, Joel, Hannah, Anne Marie,
and our new Baby Campbell soon to arrive.

OUTLINE OF THE BOOK OF JUDGES

THEME: THE PRICE OF ISRAEL'S DEPARTURE FROM GOD

I. **The Reasons for the Judges Era, 1:1–3:6**
   A. Israel's disobedience, 1:1–2:5
   B. Israel's idolatry, 2:6-19
   C. Israel's intermarriage with heathen, 2:20–3:6

II. **The Record of the Judges Era, 3:7–16:31**
   A. The first round of Israel's oppression and deliverance, 3:7-11
   B. The second round, 3:12-31
   C. The third round, 4:1–5:31
   D. The fourth round, 6:1–8:32
   E. The fifth round, 8:33–10:5
   F. The sixth round, 10:6–12:15
   G. The seventh round, 13:1–16:31

III. **The Results of the Judges Era, 17–21**
   A. Religious apostasy, 17–18
   B. Moral collapse, 19
   C. Political anarchy, 20–21

THE MAJOR JUDGES
AND THEIR
MILITARY CAMPAIGNS

Hazor•

DEBORAH
and BARAK
against the
Canaanites

Mt. Carmel ▲
Harosheth•

Ophrah•

Megiddo•

Taanach•   •Harod

GIDEON
against the Midianites

ABIMELECH

Shechem•   Succoth•   •Mahanaim
                        •
                      Penuel

Shiloh•   JEPHTHAH
                   against the
                   Ammonites

EHUD

Ekron•
Ashdod•   •Beth-shemesh

Gath•

Ashkelon•

SAMSON
against the Philistines

•Gaza   •Hebron

OTHNIEL
against King
of Mesopotamia

Miles 10 5 0   10   20
Kms 10 5 0   10   20   30

ONE

DIAGNOSIS OF A
NATIONAL DISASTER

Judges 1

The 10th anniversary of the fall of Saigon found America immersed in an introspective mood, seeking to understand at last why the most powerful nation on earth had suffered a military defeat many described as a national disaster. The American public was all but drowned under waves of words as the media interviewed Vietnam veterans, resisters, politicians, government officials, and ordinary citizens.

Israel too experienced national disaster. This national disaster, however, was not limited to one military conflict but involved many military battles, and it lasted for a period of nearly 350 years. This dark period is described in the Old Testament Book of Judges.

Judges has been called "one of the saddest books in the Bible." It records the story of a nation that had once known the wonderful works of God, a nation with a glorious history, but a nation that turned away from its grand heritage to reap a grim harvest.

This community of people had experienced God's deliverance from the bondage of Egypt, His providential care in the wilderness, and His power in giving them the land of Canaan.

But as soon as the generation witnessing these wonders died, the nation rapidly deteriorated and incurred God's great displeasure. The key, the reason for it all, is found hanging at the back door of the book: "Everyone did what was right in his own eyes" (Jud. 21:25). Even though much of their behavior was obviously evil, the Israelites rationalized their actions and justified what they did as being right. It was a permissive society to the core, a society without standards.

It would be difficult to find a section of Scripture that speaks with more relevance to our times, for we find ourselves living in a generation that has in large part rejected God's absolute standards. And leaders from various sectors of our society lament the moral decline all about us.

● Historian Arnold Toynbee stated that of the 22 civilizations appearing on the stage of world history, 19 of them collapsed when they reached the present moral condition of the United States.[1]

● In 1973 Dr. Karl Menninger wrote a book entitled *Whatever Became of Sin?* The well-known psychiatrist sensed the loss of old-fashioned morality in the unrestrained permissiveness of modern society and expressed his alarm.[2]

● Dr. Paul Saltman, professor of biology at the University of California at San Diego, declares:

> We must demand, not just of scientists but of every human being on this earth, that they begin to understand that we cannot replace the Ten Commandments with the first ten Amendments, or with ten principles of physics, and somehow come out whole. We have to demand that each person begin to understand the nature of the values and words and ethics by which he or she lives in society.[3]

● The president of Johns Hopkins University, Dr. Steven Muller, asserts:

> Failure to rally around a set of values means that we are

turning out highly skilled barbarians. Society as a whole is turning out barbarians because of the discarding of the value system it was built on. . . . To restore its lost value system, America would have to return to its faith in God. There can be no value system where there is no supreme value that transcends man's natural self-centeredness, where one man's values are esteemed as good as another's.[4]

The Book of Judges also speaks to our generation because it provides us with models of individuals who faithfully served God in dark and ugly times. Deborah, Barak, Gideon, Jephthah, and Samson are familiar names, and they conjure up for many of us memories of youthful days when we sat spellbound, listening to stories of the courageous exploits of these heroes. When the writer of the Book of Hebrews listed Old Testament characters who walked by faith in their times, he included the major judges—Gideon, Barak, Samson, and Jephthah. These men were not perfect—most of them committed grave sins; yet they were used by God, and they challenge us, with our limitations and failures, to have an impact for righteousness on our society.

The opening chapters of the Book of Judges are not happy ones. They should have been. When the wars of conquest were over, Joshua, knowing the dangers the people still faced, earnestly warned that continued obedience to God's commands was essential if they were to live in the land under His blessing. Joshua's last public act was to lead the people of Israel in a sacred ritual of covenant renewal by which they pledged to fear and follow the Lord God (Josh. 24). The Israelites returned to their homes to live "happily ever after." But it was not to be.

The very next book of Scripture reveals that instead of victory, there was defeat; instead of conquest, oppression; instead of freedom, bondage; instead of progress, decline; instead of unity, disunity; instead of a song of joy, there was a sob of sorrow. The reason is all too clear, for instead of obedience, there was disobedience; instead of faith, there was unbelief.

Some say the Book of Judges was written to explain why Israel did not receive the blessing in the land God had promised. Again, the explanation is transparent. There was disastrous failure, not on the part of God but on the part of man. The failure was both military (Jud. 1) and spiritual (Jud. 2).

The Death of Joshua

As the Book of Joshua begins with the death of the great shepherd and legislator Moses, so the Book of Judges opens with the death of Joshua, military conqueror and spiritual leader. Each death marked the end of an era—the wilderness wanderings in the one case and the wars of conquest in the other. By way of contrast, however, at the death of Moses, Joshua was already trained and ready to guide the Israelites, whereas at Joshua's death, no single, godly leader was available. Without question this void of strong leadership constitutes one explanation for the instability of the Judges period. Another factor contributing to instability was the continuing presence of pockets of resistance in the land, for though Joshua had done his job well, much territory still remained to be possessed (Josh. 13:1-7).

Does Judges 1 present a parallel but contradictory account of the conquest of Canaan as some scholars believe? Such a theory is based on the false assumption that Joshua finished the task. But as described above, Joshua did not complete the conquest. He did not, for example, capture and settle all the *cities* of the land. There is no account in Joshua of the conquest of Jerusalem, Gezer, or the five Philistine cities. Professor Yehezkel Kaufmann explains:

> This is why Joshua separates the *wars* entirely from the *occupation of the territory*. He keeps the people in *camp* for the whole duration of the war. No matter where the army fights, it always returns to the camp. Throughout the whole war Joshua does not occupy a single city, nor does he rebuild a single city. . . . He is compelled to prevent the people from occupying its portion until the

end of the war, because he cannot be sure that he will be able to muster them for the general war if they are engaged in claiming land.[5]

Occupation of the conquered territories *began*, of course, in Joshua's time (Josh. 24:28), and it *continued* after his death, according to Judges 1:1.

It was, no doubt, the influence of Joshua's last inspiring address that moved the people of Israel to ask, "Who shall go up first for us against the Canaanites to fight against them?" (Jud. 1:1)

Partial Success
in Southern and Western Canaan (1:1-20)

Who will continue to fight against the Canaanites? In keeping with the fact that Judah was appointed to leadership among the tribes, the Lord appointed her to be the first to resume the war against the Canaanites. The term *Canaanites* is used here in a broad, generic sense to describe all the inhabitants of the land west of the Jordan River. Throughout this chapter the tribes are referred to in terms of their ancestors, the sons of Jacob. Since the territory allotted to Simeon was limited to cities within Judah's territory (composed mainly of the area conquered by Joshua in his southern campaign as described in Joshua 10), it was natural that these two tribes should form an alliance against a common enemy.

Initially, Judah and Simeon enjoyed great success in their military campaigns. With God's help they won a decisive victory at *Bezek* near Jerusalem, defeating an army of 10,000 men. The Canaanite leader, Adoni-bezek, was captured and then mutilated, presumably to render him unable to use weapons in the future and to disqualify him from further royal service (Jud. 1:4-7).

Next, *Jerusalem* was taken by Judah's forces (Jud. 1:8). While some have suggested the reference here is only to a settlement on the southwest hill (modern Mount Zion), it seems best to understand this as the temporary conquest of the Jebusite capital on the Ophel (a narrow stretch of land opposite the present south wall of Jerusalem's old city). Control was soon lost (Jud. 1:21), and Jerusalem did not become Israel's permanent possession until the bold and daring conquest by David and his men about 1000 B.C. (2 Sam. 5).

A summary statement introduces the remainder of the conflicts in this region, referring to the three major geographic divisions of the territory of Judah (including Simeon) in the southern part of the land (Jud. 1:9). The first is "the hill country" or the Judean mountain range stretching over the ridge route from Jerusalem to Hebron; the second, "the Negev," is the semiarid region from just south of Hebron to Kadesh-barnea; the third, "the lowland" (literally, "the Shephelah"), is the foothills between the coastal plain and the Judean mountains, the site of frequent contests between Philistines and Israelites.

After the conquest of Jerusalem, the forces of Judah moved nineteen miles south and took *Hebron,* a city in which Abraham had lived (Gen. 13:18; 18:1; 23:2; 25:9) and which later would be David's capital during the first seven years of his reign. The leader in defeating Hebron was Caleb (Jud. 1:20; Josh. 15:14).

The next target was *Debir,* a logical quest after the fall of Hebron because it was but eleven miles southwest of that city. Othniel, who later became the first judge of Israel, assisted Caleb in the attack on Debir and, after a victorious fight, received Caleb's daughter Achsah for his wife. After the marriage, Achsah requested and received from her father "springs of water" as a bridal blessing and as compensation for the arid surroundings of her home in the Judean Negev.

Because the accounts of the capture of Hebron and Debir are also found in Joshua 15, in the context of the allotment of the tribal territories, how are we to understand the timing of these events? On the one hand it is possible that the conquests recorded in Judges 1 took place after Joshua's death with the exception of Hebron and Debir, which were conquered earlier. The translation of verse 10 would then be rendered, "So Judah *had gone* against the Canaanites who lived in Hebron." On the other hand, it is possible that the account in Judges 1 is strictly chronological, and the description of the fall of Hebron and Debir was later added to the Joshua record to give a complete picture of Judah's inheritance. This explanation then would also be true for the two accounts of the migration of the tribe of Dan (Josh. 19:47 and Jud. 18).

The account of the military successes of Judah and Simeon continues. Together they conquered and destroyed *Zephath*, believed to be about twenty miles southwest of Hebron. The city was taken and destroyed at an earlier time (Num. 21:2-3) but was rebuilt only to be retaken and "utterly destroyed." The name attached to the city, *Hormah*, is derived from a verb meaning "to devote to destruction." Once this city had been a pagan city devoted to pagan gods; now, at God's command, it was to be devoted to Him and totally destroyed.

Turning westward toward the coastal plain and attacking from the south, the men of Judah took three principal cities of the Philistines—*Gaza, Ashkelon,* and *Ekron*. Thus, at first glance it appears that Judah piled up an impressive record of military successes. On closer examination, however, we find reason to be disturbed because in the midst of success there are subtle but significant indications of failure. First is the mention of the mutilation of Adoni-bezek in verse 6. While this was an effective way to end a military career, it was nonetheless a pagan practice. Pastor Gary Inrig declares, "They were drawing their standards from people around them. And besides, God wanted these men put to death, not mutilated. The obedience of Judah was only partial."[6]

A second disturbing note is found in the words, "Now the Lord was with Judah, and they took possession of the hill country; but they could not drive out the inhabitants of the valley because they had iron chariots" (Jud. 1:19). Verse 19 does not contradict verse 18, as some suppose, for the conquered cities of Gaza, Ashkelon, and Ekron were situated in "the valley" or coastal plain. Verse 19 only indicates that after the initial victories in "the valley," the Israelites were unable to hold these cities and were forced back into the hill country where the Canaanites were unable to use chariots against them. Inrig comments,

> Judah did not drive out the Canaanites in the valley because the Canaanites had iron chariots. Now that seems logical—Judah was outgunned. But in fact, that was not the reason at all. God had promised that He would drive out the enemy. Later, in chapter 4, Deborah led Israel into victory against an army with 900 iron chariots. . . . The real reason Judah did not have victory was that they did not trust God. *Diminished power is always the result of diminished faith.*[7]

The shortfall of faith among the men of Judah paralyzed them and produced fear and retreat. God in turn called this disobedience (Jud. 2:2). Later on, David, with possible reference to the Philistines, would write, "Some boast in chariots, and some in horses; but we will boast in the name of the LORD, our God" (Ps. 20:7). Mindful of the fact that we live in an age of rising fear over the proliferation of nuclear weaponry, we would do well to ponder the wise words of Professor Arthur Cundall:

> We should all be better off today if we bore in mind that, in an age when the chariot has long since been superseded as a weapon of warfare, a faithful (and righteous) reliance upon the Lord is the stoutest weapon in the armoury of a nation or an individual.[8]

Failure at Jerusalem (1:21)

Both the tribes of Judah and Benjamin are associated with attacks on Jerusalem. Joshua 15:63 records that the sons of Judah could not conquer Jerusalem, whereas it is later recorded that Jerusalem was a city assigned to Benjamin (Josh. 18:28). After Joshua's death, Judah took Jerusalem though it was soon reoccupied (Jud. 1:8), and Benjamin thereafter failed in attempts to dislodge the Jebusites (1:21). This apparent confusion is easily explained. Because Jerusalem was situated on the tribal borders of Judah and Benjamin, both tribes felt a responsibility to expel the enemy. Both, sadly, failed. The joint failure was due to a lack of faith, not a lack of power.

Partial Success in Central Canaan (1:22-29)

Turning from south to central Canaan, we first observe that the house of Joseph, consisting of the twin tribes of Ephraim and Manasseh, won a significant victory over Bethel, twelve miles north of Jerusalem. The reason is clear—they trusted God for strength and consequently "the Lord was with them" (v. 22). Bethel was memorable to Israel as the place where God revealed Himself to the patriarch Jacob (Gen. 28:10-19).

The brief mention of success is quickly followed by a description of the failures of both tribes. In fact, a depressing catalog of uninterrupted failures sweeps through the rest of this chapter. The cities Manasseh did not capture occupied strategic locations in the valleys of Jezreel and Esdraelon, separating the tribes in central Canaan from the northern tribes. Gezer, the heavily fortified city eighteen miles northwest of Jerusalem was on the plain overlooking Joppa and guarded the pass from the coast to Jerusalem. Ephraim did not drive out the Canaanites from this strategically located city, and along with Manasseh settled for a compromise, allowing the enemy to remain in their midst, a compromise that meant ultimate catastrophe.

Failure in Northern Canaan (1:30-33)

The dreary recital continues as attention shifts northward. *Zebulun* failed to rid their territory of the Canaanites. The tribe of *Asher*, in total disobedience of God's command, apparently made little or no attempt to dislodge the Canaanites and merely moved in among them (v. 32). The price of disobedience was high. From this territory (later known as Phoenicia) came Jezebel who married Ahab and introduced Baal worship into Israel (1 Kings 16:31). The tribe of *Naphtali* similarly "lived among the Canaanites" though the inhabitants of two Canaanite strongholds, Beth-shemesh and Beth-anath, were made "forced labor" for the Israelites (vv. 28, 30, 33, 35).

Rather than obey the divine directive through Moses and Joshua to drive out the Canaanites, the Israelites chose to utilize them to increase their wealth. The far-reaching results of that decision are suggested by the names of the two cities that were spared. Beth-shemesh means "home of the sun" while Beth-anath means "house of Anath." The reference is no doubt to Canaanite shrines, the one dedicated to the worship of the sun-god, and the other dedicated to Anath, the fertility goddess and consort of Baal. One writer explains, "The emphasis is clear that idolatry remained entrenched in the land and was a problem that would ultimately destroy the moral fiber of the nation."[9]

Failure in Western Canaan (1:34-36)
The Danites, assigned a territory to the west, faced a precarious situation. Apparently they had attempted to occupy the coastal lowlands but were checked by the Amorites (synonymous here with the Canaanites) and forced to retreat to a small district in the hill country of Judah. This predicament eventually led the main body of the tribe to migrate north to Laish, near the headwaters of the Jordan (Jud. 18).

The passage before us shows a sharply deteriorating situation. In Judges 1:27-30 the Canaanites are pictured living among the Israelites and are eventually reduced to slave laborers; in verses 31-33 Asher and Naphtali live among the Canaanites, but the Canaanites dominate; finally, in verse 34 the Danites are completely dispossessed by the enemy.[10]

Becoming Uncompromising, Yielded Christians
The Israelites disobeyed God and allowed pockets of resistance to remain among them. These pockets were filled with a great infection, and the infection spread, with dire results for the body politic. Any Christian who compromises with the clear commands of Scripture faces a similar peril. Easy toleration of sin eventually leads to more serious problems.

John Hunter, Bible teacher, relates an experience at a camp meeting where Christians were invited to the front of the auditorium after the service to deal with spiritual problems.

> Among others, I knelt alongside a man more than seventy years old. He was a deacon. His silver hair made him look honorable and holy. With a broken, halting voice, and with tears streaming down his face, he poured out his soul to the Lord. His "enemy" was a dirty mind. He had a lusting desire for dirty books and pictures. The whole thing seemed so incongruous, so impossible, but it was true. He said he wanted to be used of the Lord, but all through his Christian life he had been useless—no good for God. And there was the reason. When he first trusted Christ, he allowed "the enemy" to remain. It was small and insignificant at the time, but as the many years had gone by he gradually found himself in bondage to his "enemy."[11]

Have you allowed an enemy to remain in your life? Is there some section of your heart not yielded to Christ? As believers we are called on to allow Christ as Lord to occupy every part of our lives. Paul wrote, "That [God] would grant you according to the riches of His glory, to be strengthened with power through His Spirit in the inner man; so that Christ may dwell in your hearts through faith" (Eph. 3:16-17). The last clause may also be translated, "That Christ may settle down and be at home in your hearts by faith." No one has written with more insight on the meaning and application of these words than Robert Boyd Munger in his booklet, *My Heart—Christ's Home.* He declares, "Without question one of the most remarkable Christian doctrines is that Jesus Christ Himself through the presence of the Holy Spirit will actually enter a heart, settle down, and be at home there. Christ will make the human heart His abode "[12]

TWO

WHEN MEN FORGOT GOD

Judges 2

Alexander Solzhenitsyn, in a noted address, reflects on the tragedies that have overtaken his country.

> Over half a century ago, while I was still a child, I recall hearing a number of older people offer the following explanation for the great disasters that had befallen Russia: "Men have forgotten God; that's why all of this has happened." Since then I have spent well-nigh fifty years working on the history of our revolution; in the process I have read hundreds of books, collected hundreds of personal testimonies, and have already contributed eight volumes of my own toward the effort of clearing away the rubble left by that upheaval. But if I were asked today to formulate as concisely as possible the main cause of the ruinous revolution that swallowed up some sixty million of our people, I could not put it more accurately than to repeat: "Men have forgotten God; that's why all this has happened."[1]

Anyone seeking an explanation for the great disasters that

befell Israel during the period of the Judges need not look beyond this—men forgot God. The inspired historian wrote, "The sons of Israel . . . forgot the LORD their God" (Jud. 3:7).

The Lord confronted the people of Israel with their spiritual failure in chapter 2 of the Book of Judges. It is a vigorous and pointed indictment of the nation God had chosen.

The Disobedience of Israel (2:1-5)

The angel of the Lord came from Gilgal, Israel's first encampment near Jericho, to Bochim (literally, "the weepers"). (Bochim could possibly be identified with the "oak of weeping" near Bethel, mentioned in Genesis 35:8.) The importance of this event is underscored by the fact that the Lord Himself appeared to face His people with the undeniable evidence of their infidelity. The angel of the Lord is identified in Scripture as a theophany, an appearance of God in visible and bodily form. He appeared thus to Joshua (Josh. 5:13-15) and would later appear to Gideon (Jud. 6:11-24) and to the parents of Samson (Jud. 13:3-21).

The Lord reminded the people that He had redeemed them out of Egypt and had established a covenant with them requiring that they make no treaty with the Canaanites and that they avoid the idolatry of the land. The Israelites failed on both counts: they made a covenant with the inhabitants of Canaan (Josh. 9:1-27; Jud. 1:28, 30, 33), and they failed to destroy the pagan altars. The Lord allowed for no excuses or rationalizations but charged Israel with blatant disobedience and thus asked the searching question, "Why have you done this?" (Jud. 2:2, NIV) It was a question spoken in grace, designed to bring the sinning Israelites to repentance.

A parent addresses the same question to an erring child with the purpose of producing in that child a change of heart. But the people of Israel were silent; they had no answer or perhaps they dared not voice the real truth. John Hunter explains it well:

No, the awful truth of the reason why they had not

driven out the inhabitants and destroyed their altars and their worship was simply this: they did not want to drive them out. They chose to allow these people with their evil, lustful ways to remain. Something in God's people wanted what they saw in that world. Their fallen human nature responded to the wild degrading dances of the heathen worship. The prospect of involvement with male and female prostitutes made their blood tingle with excitement. That was a totally new way of life and all that was in them cried out for this new culture. So it was that no one drove out anyone.[2]

In the face of such stark failure, God affirmed two things:
1. "I will never break My covenant with you" (Jud. 2:1) The divine promise was true not only in this situation, but has remained true from that time to the present. However deeply Israel has sinned, God has never broken His covenant with her
2. "I will not drive them out before you" (Jud. 2:3). Though God remains faithful to His covenant promises to Israel, her sins will always bring divine chastisement. (See the description of the Davidic covenant in 2 Samuel 7:12-16.) In this case the Lord declared He would not drive out the Canaanites, but instead they would become as thorns in the sides of the Israelites.

Hearing these stern words of judgment, the people wept and then offered sacrifices. But in the light of what soon followed, we must conclude that the tears were more signs of regret for the penalty than tears of repentance for the sin. The sacrifices too were apparently only an empty ritual. As one author states, "True repentance must go beyond tears of sorrow and achieve a right-about-face, a turning of one's entire life from sin to a walk that pleases the Lord."[3]

The Spiritual Indifference of Israel (2:6-10)

As an introduction to the distressing development ahead for Israel, the writer provides us with a review of the days of Joshua and the elders (vv. 6-9), a transition to the new generation

(v. 10), and a preview of the period of the Judges (vv. 11-19). Judges 2:6-9 is paralleled in Joshua 24:28-31 where it is emphasized that the Israelites were faithful to the Lord throughout the lifetime of Joshua and the elders who outlived him. This is attributed to the fact that that generation had firsthand, experiential knowledge of the great acts of God—the deliverance from Egypt, the miraculous crossings of the Red Sea and Jordan River, and the victories in the wars of conquest.

Tribute must also be paid to the influence of Joshua, a great soldier and dynamic leader, called here simply "the servant of the Lord" (Jud. 2:8). This godly man of faith had a tremendous influence on his times, extending even beyond his death. In this he stands as a model for today's Christian:

> One man, committed unreservedly to God and His Word, can make an enormous difference for good in the lives of God's people. One woman, living her life for Jesus Christ, can bring blessing to a whole group of people. If you will trust God and build your life on His Word, you can have a godly influence on your family, student group, or local church. That truth is written many times on the pages of Scripture.[4]

The new generation is then introduced and the situation changes—for the worse. "And there arose another generation after them who did not know the LORD, nor yet the work which He had done for Israel" (Jud. 2:10). How could it happen? Who was to blame?

One cold spring I held a Bible conference in a mainline denominational church in the far north of our country. The church had a great spiritual heritage, but I soon observed that the audience was composed almost exclusively of older people. When I asked the assistant pastor about the absence of younger people, he could only reply, "The next generation is simply not interested in spiritual things!" Who was responsible for this sad state of affairs?

In 1 Samuel 2:12 it is recorded, "Now the sons of Eli were

worthless men; they did not know the Lord." Who was to blame?

With reference to the Judges' situation, many are quick to blame the parents, the first generation, assuming that they failed to carry out the charge of Deuteronomy 6:7-8, 20-25 to pass spiritual truth on to their children. Declares one writer, "Apparently Israel had failed to discharge this responsibility, and the result was a godless generation."[5] While such an explanation may account in part for the spiritual indifference of the new generation, the Scriptures do not put the blame there. Rather, the second generation was held responsible for their own spiritual apostasy and judged accordingly. They were not permitted to shift the blame to anyone else. Furthermore, the description of the second generation as a generation "who did not know the Lord" (Jud. 2:10), may be understood in the sense of not acknowledging Him; thus the failure was due more to their indifference or unbelief than to mere ignorance of spiritual truth.

Often, Christian parents are consumed with guilt over wayward children because they assume the full responsibility to produce dedicated Christian sons and/or daughters. After all, doesn't the Bible promise, "Train up a child in the way he should go, even when he is old he will not depart from it"? (Prov. 22:6) But considering the entire content of the Book of Proverbs leads us to the conclusion that the verse cited is more a principle than a promise. It explains what normally happens, i.e., good parenting usually produces good children. The Book of Proverbs describes both obedient sons who prosper and disobedient sons who court tragedy.

Dr. John White, counselor and professor of psychiatry, in his insightful book, *Parents in Pain*, states:

> I have never counted the number of verses about good sons or stacked them up against the number of verses about bad or good parents, but the book deals with both. As we look at it as a whole we begin to see why "Instruct a child in the way he should go . . ." is not

meant to be an inflexible law. Parents are admonished to bring up their children properly. Children are admonished to respond wisely to parental correction. If both play their part, all will be well. But it takes a parent-child team working in harmony to produce this happy result. Good parenting is part, perhaps the major part of the story; but a great deal of emphasis is placed on attentive obedient children who listen and welcome the correction of their parents.[6]

Some have described Israel's lack of response to the Lord as an illustration of the "second-generation syndrome—a lukewarmness, a complacency, an apathy about amazing biblical truths. The second generation was satisfied with the status quo, took God's blessings for granted refusing to acknowledge Him, and neglected God's Word."[7]

The lesson is profound. The spiritual experience of our generation cannot automatically be passed on to the next. The responsibility of each generation of believers is to build on the foundation of the past. The key to the period of the Judges was the failure of Israel to make an inherited faith a personal faith.

The Apostasy, Punishment, and Deliverance of Israel (2:11-19)

A preview of the Judges period is now set before us as the history of over three centuries is summarized. The recurring pattern of events is illustrated throughout the narratives of the main judges. The cycle included five phases (though not all are included in this summary passage):

1. rebellion or apostasy;
2. retribution or chastisement;
3. repentance or supplication;
4. restoration or deliverance;
5. rest or a period of peace.[8]

The *rebellion* of Israel is graphically described in Judges 2, verses 11-13. The sin is so grievous that the inspired historian repeats the charge of transgression three times in three verses.

This second generation, which was apathetic and indifferent to the faith of their fathers, now turned its back on the true God of their fathers to serve the false gods of Canaan. The magnitude of this sin can only be understood against the background of God's grace in delivering these people from Egypt and bringing them into a national homeland, a "land that flowed with milk and honey." They shamelessly abandoned this God of grace and bowed down to gods of filth and uncleanness. Specifically, we are told, they worshiped and served Baal and Ashtaroth, false deities in the Canaanite pantheon of gods.

Baal was the god of the storm who rode upon the clouds and was responsible for the crop-watering rains. Ashtaroth, Baal's consort, was the goddess of war and fertility. The sexual union of these gods in the heavens was thought to result in abundant harvests of crops on earth. Furthermore, the followers of Baal and Ashtaroth believed in sympathetic magic, that is, they felt that to ensure large crops they must behave as the gods. The resultant worship involved temple prostitution, debased fertility rites, drunken sexual orgies, etc. The Israelites succumbed to this strong, sensuous appeal and fell headlong into the sin of idolatry.

The *retribution* of God described in verses 14 and 15 summarizes God's repeated judgments on Israel during the long period of the Judges. God's anger against His people needs no justification. Idolatry and its accompanying immorality were totally incompatible with the covenant relationship between God and Israel (Ex. 20:2-5; Lev. 19:2-4). Consequently, He used Israel's enemies on all sides to chastise this rebellious people. The psalmist provides a vivid picture of Israel's rebellious ways and resultant sufferings at the hand of God (Ps. 106:34-45).

The *repentance* of the Israelites and their supplication for deliverance from the painful yokes of oppression is not specifically stated here. We know, however, from the narratives of the main judges that the Lord responded because Israel repented and turned to God (Jud. 3:9, 15; 4:3; 6:6-7; 10:10). Such repentance may be alluded to in the words, "for the LORD was moved to pity by their groaning because of those who oppressed and afflicted them" (Jud. 2:18).

The *restoration* of Israel is portrayed in verses 16-18. When Israel turned to God, He intervened to deliver them. It has been said that the Book of Judges provides a "miniature history of man, the story of our human race with its ups and downs, triumphs and tragedies. But it is also the revelation of divine intervention in the affairs of mankind."⁹

The Book of Judges thus gives us some interesting insights into a biblical as opposed to a pagan philosophy of history. For the most part, the ancient historians were only annalists or chroniclers. The Greeks, for example, had a cyclical view of history. They believed events occurred in endless cycles and that each succeeding generation did the same things the previous generation did. History had no goal and no meaning. Such a view produced a fatalistic attitude toward life. More recently, another view of history has been propounded by the existentialists. For them history is without meaning and is only a succession of events with no significance.

The biblical view of history is different. It reveals that God has purposes in history and that history is moving toward the grand goal of the reign of Christ on earth. God will intervene in the future to bring this about just as He intervened in the past to deal with the nations and His chosen people. God is not an "absentee landlord," and the universe is not a closed system defying His intervention. Nor is history drifting aimlessly along without design or purpose. God intervened in the period of the Judges to judge evil and reward the righteous, and the Bible predicts He will do the same on some unsuspecting tomorrow. Peter prophesies that in spite of the mockers who ask, "Where is the [fulfillment of the] promise of His coming?" the "day of the LORD will come like a thief, in which the heavens will pass away with a roar and the elements will be destroyed with intense heat, and the earth and its works will be burned up" (2 Peter 3:4, 10).

Following a message I delivered on God's purposes and plans for the world and for us as His children, I received the following letter from the mother of a large family.

The news reports don't usually "get to me" because God is always reminding me of His goodness and love toward me. It's also comforting to know that He is sovereign. But, the latter part of last week the evil seemed overwhelming. The newscasts seemed unbelievable. Your message yesterday was just what God wanted me to hear. Lawlessness will increase but God is still in control and He wants me to live a godly life!

Lawlessness and wickedness prevailed in the time of the judges. But who were these "judges" raised up by a gracious, intervening God to deliver a sinful but repentant people? Are we to think in terms of 20th-century models, of dignified individuals in dark robes who preside in solemn courtrooms? Actually, the judges of this Old Testament period would share little more than the name in common with our 20th-century judges. Primarily, they were saviors or deliverers, men (and one woman) who could plan military strategy and raise and lead an army. They were individuals selected by God in emergency times for specific service, but there was no ruling family or line of succession. Furthermore, these people possessed good judgment, were able to give wise counsel, and championed legal and political rights. Finally, they had a spiritual relationship with God and were blessed and led by Him. In confirmation of this we find in Judges 2:18 that:

1. judges were raised up by the LORD;
2. the LORD was with them;
3. the LORD used them to deliver Israel.

The question may be asked, "Why did God repeatedly raise up the judges?" The question is particularly appropriate in the light of Judges 2:17, 19 where it is revealed that the Israelites did not heed their judges but "turned aside quickly from the way in which their fathers had walked." Furthermore, after the death of the judge "they would turn back and act more corruptly. . . they did not abandon their practices or their stubborn ways." Throughout the period there was a progressive deterioration, "each successive cycle being characterized by a greater descent into apostasy and corruption, and by a more superficial repentance, than the one preceding."[10] The only explanation for the provision of judges or deliverers is to be found in the character of God, for while this book tells us much about the evil heart of man it correspondingly reveals much about God—His faithfulness, forbearance, love, and grace. According to Cundall, "His grace strikes a glad note in this book which cannot be silenced by the discordant notes which appear to predominate."[11]

An old Indian chief, after living many years in sin, was led to Christ by a missionary. Friends asked him to explain the change in his life. Reaching down, he picked up a little worm and placed it on a pile of leaves. Then, touching a match to the leaves, he watched them smolder and burst into flames. As the flames worked their way up to the center where the worm lay, the old chief suddenly plunged his hand into the center of the burning pile and snatched the worm out. Holding the worm gently in his hand, he gave this testimony to the grace of God: "Me . . . that worm!" So is the grace of God seen in the history of Israel and in the life of each believer who has been delivered "from the domain of darkness and transferred . . . to the kingdom of His beloved Son" (Col. 1:13).

The Divine Testing of Israel (2:20-23)

This section provides a fitting conclusion to the dreary recital of human failure for it discloses the divine purpose in the dark circumstances in which Israel found herself. The psalmist declared, "For the wrath of man shall praise Thee" (Ps. 76:10). So here we discover how Israel's failure to drive out the Canaanites would be used by God to accomplish His purpose for the nation.

Israel, the Lord declared, had broken the covenant—a reference to the Mosaic code given at Sinai, the human side of which required obedience and fidelity. To punish the Israelites for their transgression (Jud. 2:11-19), the Lord declared He would no longer drive out the Canaanites. This was in keeping with the warning delivered to their forefathers (Josh. 23:12-

13). We should observe that the previous section speaks of foreign nations invading and plundering Israel, whereas the reference here is to Canaanite peoples already in the land who had not been displaced by Israel. These Canaanites would also be divine instruments to chastise Israel for her apostasy in embracing idolatry.

This section of Scripture also reveals that God's purpose in allowing the Canaanites to remain was to test the faithfulness of the generations that followed Joshua. Would they "keep the way of the Lord to walk in it as their fathers did or not"? (Jud. 2:22)

It was a searching test, a veritable ordeal by fire, and for the most part Israel failed to pass. Yet the periodic long periods of rest from divine chastisement reflect the fact that some learned the lesson God was teaching.

Thus, we see that God permitted the Israelites to fall into straits from which they could not be delivered apart from His intervention. They were thereby forced to acknowledge the true God and seek His help. So it is with His people today.

> God knows how prone we are to lose sight of Him when we do not seem to need Him, and to forget Him when things are going well. He therefore often allows adversaries to stand in our way: a sick baby, an unfair employer, an unpleasant neighbor, an unfaithful friend—in order to keep us close to Himself.[12]

A former colleague at our Seminary who had been a pastor told the poignant story of a grieving father who one Sunday morning asked the pastor if he would go to the hospital with him and tell his wife that the baby born to them the previous night was hopelessly retarded. The minister did so, explaining that the child, if he lived, would be helpless and totally dependent on his parents for all his needs.

The parents reacted to the situation by sacrificially and lovingly caring for their only child all his life of over thirty years. On occasion they became indignant when hospital care was needed, and some doctors did not want to give medical help When the child was still young, the pastor called on the father in his art studio. Pointing to the helpless infant in his nearby crib, the father said, "Pastor, the Lord had to give me that child to bring me to Himself."

C.S. Lewis explains, "God whispers in our pleasures, speaks in our conscience, but shouts in our pains: it is His megaphone to rouse a deaf world."[13] God used affliction to get the attention of Israel. He still uses suffering to keep us trusting Himself.

THREE
FREEDOM FIGHTERS
Judges 3

Years of peace for the entire world have been few and far between. Names of great battles and renowned military heroes fill the history books and remind us of tragic events. But many of the heroes are unnamed. They went to their graves early and unacclaimed.

In a recent trip to the mission fields of the Third World (better called the Two-Thirds world because of its massive population), my wife and I were profoundly moved as we visited the American military cemetery in Manila. Immaculately kept, it contains the graves of some 18,000 Americans who died in World War II and memorializes an additional 17,000 MIAs. The previous week we had stood before a magnificent monument in Malaysia's capital city, Kuala Lumpur. Victorious Malaysian freedom fighters were portrayed standing over their fallen enemies. Inscribed in golden letters were the words, "Dedicated to the heroic fighters in the cause of peace and freedom."

The times make the hero, it has been said. As recorded in Judges 3, the heroes began to emerge in a time of turbulence previously unknown in Israel's history. The opening chapters of the book provide the reasons for such chaos, and now the focus is on the record of Israel's recurring failures and God's repeated chastisements. The judges played a significant role as God's instruments to deliver a repentant Israel from oppression. They too were dedicated to the cause of peace and freedom. They too were freedom fighters.

Enemy Nations in the Land (3:1-6)

Before rehearsing the gripping stories of particular judges, the writer of the Book of Judges lists the nations that remained in Canaan—nations that had not been conquered by Joshua and that would not be permanently driven out by the exploits of the judges (vv. 3, 5). He then discusses further the divine purpose in these circumstances, namely, to test the obedience and faith of the Israelites (Jud. 2:22) and to give this generation experience in the art of warfare, that is, the kind of "holy warfare" associated with Joshua's conquest of Canaan. Cundall explains:

> Israel was to be in a hostile environment for the major part of her history, due either to the pressures of the petty kingdoms which surrounded her or, at a later stage, due to her strategic position between the successive world-powers of Assyria, Babylonia, Persia and Greece on the one hand and Egypt on the other hand. Military prowess was a necessary accomplishment, humanly speaking, if she was to survive. And yet the attainment of this prowess only rarely obscured the fact that the victory was not the result of their own might but of the Lord's working for them (e.g., 2 Sam. 8:6, 14).[1]

The other side of the story is that the sinful failure of Israel in not driving out the pagan peoples of Canaan left them surrounded by temptations too great for them to bear. The Canaanite religion with its nature gods and associated corrupt practices repeatedly swept them off their feet so that generation after generation forsook the faith of their fathers. The progres-

sion downward is pointedly described in verses 5 and 6:
1. the Israelites "lived among the Canaanites";
2. they intermarried with the Canaanites;
3. they served the Canaanite gods.
Yet God in grace did not utterly forsake His people. He never does.

Othniel vs. Cushan-rishathaim of Mesopotamia (3:7-11)

Moving from the general to the particular, we come to the first specific account of Israel's apostasy, chastisement, and deliverance. Seven such accounts are spread over Judges 3–16 and provide an insightful commentary on the political and spiritual fortunes of Israel during the fourteenth and thirteenth centuries B.C. As noted in the previous chapter, each cycle follows a common pattern of spiritual rebellion, divine retribution, national repentance, restoration through a divinely appointed judge, and a period of rest before the next cycle begins.

Rebellion (3:7). Influenced by their Canaanite neighbors who were also in some cases family members, the Israelites deliberately shut the Lord out of their minds and turned to worship and serve the Baals and the Asheroth, the male and female vegetation deities of the land. The term *Asheroth* is a plural of *Asherah* and apparently refers to a wooden pillar or tree trunk considered a dwelling place of a deity. In this case that deity was a Canaanite goddess named Asherah, referred to in the Ras Shamra tablets as the consort of the supreme god, El, and mother of the gods.

Worshiping the Baals and Asheroth violated the first two commandments (Ex. 20:3-6), and this blatant disobedience by Israel of the divine law did not escape God's notice. This evil was in fact done "in the sight of the LORD" (Jud. 3:7). Every deed of man is done in the full view of God. To think otherwise is to deny implicitly or explicitly that God is omniscient and therefore knows all things and to deny that He is omnipresent and therefore sees all things.

Perhaps Israel reasoned like the young man who came to counsel with a faculty member at our seminary about his marital problems. After pouring out his problems, he said, "We sure don't want the Lord to know about this!" But the Lord already knew, for He heard every word and had observed every misdeed.

Dr. Lewis Sperry Chafer related to a seminary theology class many years ago how he startled his church audience one Sunday with the words, "Secret sin on earth is open scandal in heaven!" The obvious discomfort of a number of individuals betrayed the fact that they were engaged in activities they realized God would not approve of. God is righteous and will not long tolerate sin on the part of His people.

Retribution (3:8). God loved the people of Israel, but He hated their sin. His anger was kindled like a fire and burned against His people. One writer explains,

> We do not usually think of God as "getting mad." This is beneath the divine nature and dignity. Yet the righteous indignation of godly men gives us an insight into the revulsion which God feels when confronted with sin. A beloved and saintly minister once arose in a presbytery meeting to protest against an impending motion. "That makes my Anglo-Saxon blood boil," he shouted, and men thought the more of him for his anger.[2]

Israel often experienced the wrath of God throughout her history. The psalmist would later reflect on this fact and poignantly express awareness of God's anger, "All our days pass away under Your wrath" (Ps. 90:9, NIV). The writer to the Hebrews declared, "For we know Him who said, 'VENGEANCE IS MINE, I WILL REPAY.' And again, 'THE LORD WILL JUDGE HIS PEOPLE!' It is a terrifying thing to fall into the hands of the living God" (Heb. 10:30-31). The most famous and perhaps most effective sermon delivered by Jonathan Edwards was on this theme and was entitled, "Sinners in the Hands of an Angry God."

Israel felt the heat of God's anger as He sold the nation into the hands of a foreign conqueror, Cushan-rishathaim. By means of this transaction, Israel was given entirely over to the power of her enemies (Jud. 2:14; 4:2; 10:7). The Israelites had refused to serve the righteous and holy God, and now they were forced to serve a cruel and evil taskmaster whose name means "Cushan of double wickedness." Perhaps this name was ascribed to the king by others who had suffered under his yoke. Now Israel would share that experience for eight long, hard years.

The conqueror came from Mesopotamia or Aram-naharaim, literally "Syria of the Two Rivers." Some Bible scholars have thought it strange that a monarch from the far north should invade and plunder Israel in the south, and especially Judah, where Othniel lived. But invasions from Mesopotamia were not unknown in biblical times as the foray of Chedorlaomer as far south as Sodom demonstrates (Gen. 14). It is likely that Cushan-rishathaim marched his army down the King's Highway, through Trans-Jordan, and then circled south of the Dead Sea to invade Judah and enslave the backslidden people there for eight years.

Repentance (3:9). Finally, the Israelites had had enough. They learned by experience that the way of the transgressor is hard. How foolish they had been to think they must adopt Baal worship in order to prosper in the new land. Had not Yahweh promised fertility, prosperity, and security to His people when they obeyed His commandments? (Deut. 28:1-12) By turning away from the God of Israel, they had brought upon themselves curses instead of blessings (Deut. 28:15-19). Now Israel came to her spiritual senses and called on the Lord in repentance. Distress drove them to prayer. It usually does. The Lord heard, and though He could have justly ignored them, He was moved with compassion for His oppressed people and raised up a deliverer.

Restoration (3:9-10). Othniel, Israel's first liberator in this dark age, was an extraordinary person. Some consider him to be the most outstanding of all the judges. It is noteworthy that the biblical writer records no negative traits about him. As a nephew, or preferably younger brother, of Caleb, he had apparently been greatly influenced by this man who "followed the LORD fully" (Num. 14:24; Deut. 1:36).

Othniel was also a good choice because he was no novice in warfare. He had volunteered to fight the Anakim at Debir where he won a decisive victory (Jud. 1:11-15). Now, some thirty years later, Othniel recruited an army, equipped and trained his soldiers in enemy-occupied territory, and led his men to victory against a better trained and equipped enemy force.

The victory over Cushan-rishathaim, however, did not come simply because Othniel had military experience and skills. The true key to the success of this and any leader is supernatural enablement. Othniel triumphed in battle because "the Spirit of the LORD came upon him" (Jud. 3:10), empowering him to achieve what he could not have done unaided. So the Spirit also empowered Gideon (6:34), Jephthah (11:29), and Samson (13:25; 14:6, 19; 15:14), emphasizing the need for the intervention of God and His provision of power and wisdom to fight against overwhelming odds. These and other Old Testament references imply the temporary ministry of the Holy Spirit; in that age He empowered individuals for specific tasks. Since Pentecost, the Holy Spirit indwells all believers permanently (John 14:16; Eph. 4:30).

Othniel not only "went out to war," but he also "judged Israel." Thus the functions of the office of judge are clearly delineated: judges had both a civil and a military responsibility. While the latter function is given more prominence in the Book of Judges, the civil function should not be overlooked. In this capacity the judges ruled without reigning. They did not make new laws or impose new taxes. But like Moses and Joshua before them, they heard and decided on the greater causes, providing advice and arbitration when tribes or individuals appealed to them.

Rest (3:11). Following Othniel's God-given victory over Cushan-rishathaim, there was rest for an entire generation of forty years. No doubt the godly leadership of Othniel continued for much, if not all, of this period. The Israelites, having served Baal and Cushan-rishathaim, now affirmed with Joshua of old,

"As for me and my house, we will serve the LORD" (Josh. 24:15). As a result, for this generation at least, there was peace in the land.

Ranked first among the judges by Jewish rabbis, Othniel has much to teach us. He was a brave and valiant man who was willing to undertake hard and even dangerous assignments for God: as a young man, he fought giants at Debir; as an older man he moved against the powerful Aramaeans. He was also a man of faith. At Kadesh-barnea he heard his older brother Caleb exhort the Israelites not to fear the giants in Canaan but to trust the Lord. Caleb said, "The LORD is with us; do not fear them" (Num. 14:9). This became the watchword of Othniel's life as he made his brother's faith his own. This was the man God used in Israel's dark hour. He models for us the type of person God uses today.

Ehud vs. Eglon of Moab (3:12-30)

Rebellion (3:12a). The second cycle of Israel's apostasy is described by the distressing words, "Now the sons of Israel again did evil in the sight of the LORD." This grievous refrain blots the pages of the Book of Judges seven times (2:11; 3:7, 12; 4:1; 6:1; 10:6; 13:1), pointedly underscoring the charge of the Prophet Jeremiah: "The heart is more deceitful than all else and is desperately sick; who can understand it?" (Jer. 17:9) The deepening depravity of the new generation is apparent as they "turned aside quickly" from the faith of their fathers and acted even "more corruptly" in worshiping and serving other gods (Jud. 2:17, 19).

Retribution (3:12b-14). The chastisement of the Lord was not long in coming. This time, God in His sovereignty chose to use Moab to punish Israel. Throughout the Old Testament period, God used pagan rulers to accomplish His purposes. An Assyrian king is described as "the rod of My anger" (Isa. 10:5), and Cyrus of Persia was an instrument in God's hands (Isa. 45:1). The Lord said, "For I will strengthen the arms of the king of Babylon and put My sword in his hand; and I will break the arms of Pharaoh" (Ezek. 30:24). Cundall comments on these demonstrations of God's sovereignty: "It is a comforting thought in these days of nuclear power to realize God still orders and controls the destinies of nations and overrules the decisions of world rulers, including the most arrogant and atheistic among them."[3]

The Moabites were descendants of Lot through an incestuous union with his daughter (Gen. 19:30-38). The land of Moab was east of the Dead Sea, but the Moabites had apparently expanded their borders in Trans-Jordan by defeating the eastern tribes of Reuben, Gad, and the half tribe of Manasseh. Strong enough to force an alliance with the Ammonites, their northeastern neighbors, and the Amalekites, nomads of the Negev country south of Beersheba, Moab and her allies swept across the Jordan River following Joshua's route of the conquest of central Canaan. Quickly defeating Israel's feeble resistance, the enemy set up headquarters in the city of palm trees, Jericho. While most assume that Jericho had been reoccupied but not refortified because of Joshua's curse (Josh. 6:26), it is more probable that the site had lain desolate since Joshua's time. Eglon saw that this was a strategic location from which he could control much of central Canaan. There was an ample water supply. Using the rubble of the ruined city, he apparently erected a building to serve as his headquarters. Archaeologists Garstang and Kenyon date the foundation of a building on Tell Jericho to the time of Eglon's oppression, suggesting it may have been the structure used by the Moabite king.[4]

The Moabite presence in Israel was onerous, yet it continued for eighteen years because the Israelites persisted in their idolatrous ways, stubbornly refusing to repent and return to Yahweh.

Repentance (3:15a). At last the Israelites faced up to the harsh realities of living under God's discipline. With repentant hearts they cried out for mercy, and God heard them.

The psalmist reflected on the sins of these people who were polluting the land with idolatrous practices:

> Therefore the anger of the LORD was kindled against
> His people,

And He abhorred His inheritance.
Then He gave them into the hand of the nations;
And those who hated them ruled over them.
Their enemies also oppressed them,
And they were subdued under their power.
Many times He would deliver them;
They, however, were rebellious in their counsel,
And so sank down in their iniquity.
Nevertheless He looked upon their distress,
When He heard their cry;
And He remembered His covenant for their sake,
And relented according to the greatness of His
    loving-kindness.

                            (Ps. 106:40-45)

Restoration (3:15b-29). Ehud of the tribe of Benjamin is the God-appointed deliverer. He will do for Benjamin and the central tribes what Othniel accomplished for Judah in the south. Specific mention is made of the fact that Ehud was left-handed (literally, "restricted as to his right hand"). Considered a physical defect in ancient Israel, it seems to have been common among Benjamites, who nonetheless were celebrated warriors (Jud. 20:16). Ehud took what some considered a defect and turned it into a tool to be used for God. Specifically, Ehud's left-handedness provided him with the opportunity to plan and execute the assassination of the hated Moabite king, Eglon. Gary Inrig observes, "Many of us are defeated by things in our lives which may be no more significant than left-handedness. But if we do not accept our limitations, they can keep us from being usable. When we accept ourselves with our weaknesses and limitations, God can use us."[5]

When someone asked Hudson Taylor why he was chosen to lead the great China Inland Mission, he said, "God chose me because I was weak enough. God does not do His great works by large committees. He trains someone to be quiet enough and little enough, and then He uses him."

An annual tribute was laid on the Israelites by Eglon and no doubt consisted of silver, gold, cattle, and produce. Ehud was selected to lead the bearers to Eglon at his capital, perhaps Medeba. In preparation for his assassination plot, he made a dagger, which he strapped to his right thigh where there was less likelihood of its discovery in case of a search and from which position he could swiftly draw it with his left hand.

Ehud and his companions journeyed to Moab, delivered the tribute to Eglon, "a very fat man," and then left to return home. Puzzling to many, however, is the fact that at Gilgal, Ehud abruptly left the bearers and returned to the palace of Eglon alone, seeking a private audience with the king. It should be understood that Ehud first stood before the king in an official capacity. Now that the official delegation had returned to Israel, Ehud could return in a private capacity to carry out the bold plot he had secretly conceived. Furthermore, on the occasion of the delivery of the tribute, the court would have been crowded with enough armed Moabite soldiers to impress Ehud and his company of their military power. No opportunity would be present to assassinate the king, and any attempt to have done so would have been fatal for the Israelites.

Is there significance to the fact that Ehud paused and then turned back to Moab at the idols (actually—"the sculptured stones") near Gilgal? Remember that Gilgal was a sacred location where the stones set up by Joshua commemorated the miraculous Jordan crossing (Josh. 4:19-24). Perhaps these "sculptured stones" were the very ones placed there by Joshua. It also may be that at this revered place Ehud received a message from God.

Returning again to Moab, Ehud gained a private audience with Eglon and announced to the king, "I have a message from God for you" (Jud. 3:20). Ancient monarchs were always eager to receive favorable oracles from the gods, and Eglon was no exception. Laboriously arising from his seat to receive the divine message, he met Ehud, who, with a quick maneuver he had rehearsed often, drew the dagger and plunged it into the corpulent king. The "message" for Eglon was contained in the words of promise to Abraham and his descendants, "I will bless

those who bless you, *and the one who curses you I will curse"*
(Gen. 12:3, emphasis added).

Leaving Eglon dying on the floor of his upper chamber, Ehud
locked the doors behind him and casually walked out of the
palace. The king's servants may have observed him leave but
saw no cause for suspicion. Even when they discovered the
doors to the upper chamber locked, they assumed the king was
in his bathroom. Much later, after Ehud was safely out of the
region, the servants opened the doors, looked in on a bloody
scene, and saw their ruler stretched out on the floor dead.

Ehud meanwhile had made good his escape and returned to
the hill country of Ephraim where he blew the trumpet and
issued a call to arms. Sensing this was the moment of opportunity to cast off the yoke of Moab, he speedily gathered an army,
captured the fords of the Jordan opposite Moab, and killed
10,000 Moabites there who were desperately seeking an escape
route to return to their own country. So decisive was the defeat
that the Moabites became "subject to Israel" (Jud. 3:30, NIV).

Rest (3:30). Once again, the Israelites learned their lesson.
After eighteen years of Moabite oppression and bondage, they
determined to turn from their idolatry and follow the Lord God
of Israel wholeheartedly. The result was eighty years of freedom
and peace, the longest period of rest in the entire period of the
judges.

Ehud is a controversial biblical character. Some disapprove of
his actions, stating that we are not called to admire his cold-
blooded assassination of Eglon. Others excuse his deed on the
grounds that the judges were cast in the mold of their time.
Still others find much to admire in a man who lacked the
refinement and spiritual qualities of Othniel but was nonetheless used by God. He was daring, bold, efficient, and fully
determined to carry out the mission to which God had called
him, i.e., to deliver Israel from the oppressing Moabites. The
thoroughness with which he performed his task explains in part
the extended period of peace that followed.

While Ehud may not have been the spiritual leader his prede-
cessor was (it is not recorded that the Spirit of the Lord came

upon him), he was fully aware that it was not his ability or cleverness that brought victory but the power of God. His battle cry to the Ephramites at the Jordan fords was, "Pursue them, for the LORD has given your enemies the Moabites into your hands" (3:28). This conviction is essential for leadership in the work of God.

Shamgar vs. the Philistines (3:31)

Very brief mention is made of the deliverer Shamgar. He appears somewhat parenthetically between the extended accounts of the exploits of Ehud and Deborah. Many of the features common to the judges narratives are missing in connection with Shamgar, yet his exploits called for special mention in the sacred text. Indeed, there is ample evidence that he is to be considered a judge, though a minor one by comparison.

It appears that Shamgar's judgeship developed during the extended period of peace following Ehud's deliverance and before Ehud's death, recorded in Judges 4:1. It was a time when the Philistines were a threat to Judah, and Shamgar was sent by God to meet that threat and deliver His people.

Shamgar's family background is perplexing. His name is non-Israelite in origin, and his father's name, Anath, is also the name of the Canaanite goddess of sex and war. It may be that Shamgar was a Canaanite convert from raw paganism to the worship of the true God, or his father's name may show how deeply paganism influenced this Israelite family.

Only one of Shamgar's episodes is recorded, but it is noteworthy. He killed 600 Philistines with an ox goad. This figure may actually represent the number of people Shamgar killed in a lifetime, not in a single encounter. His only weapon was an ox goad, a heavy, spear-like instrument with a spike at one end to prod cattle and a blade for scraping a plowshare on the other end. Perhaps Shamgar chose this unusual weapon because it would disarm the Philistines who would not expect an attack from a person carrying an agricultural implement.

Although the main Philistine oppression of Israel would come at a later time (Jud. 13–16), the threat was sufficient at this time for alarm, and God raised up a deliverer who "saved Israel" (3:31).

Shamgar was a man of humble background, a peasant farmer, who used a humble weapon to carry out an important mission. He was courageous and a capable warrior, and it may be assumed he trusted God to enable him for this task. Perhaps his exploits were an encouragement to Samson when he later faced the same enemy. Shamgar's story illustrates how God sometimes uses the humblest of instruments to accomplish His purposes.

The three "freedom fighters" of this chapter clearly reveal that God uses people of outstanding ability and spirituality (Othniel); people who have obvious defects or limitations (Ehud); and people of lowly background (Shamgar). No believer need feel useless because God has a ministry for each one. The requirement for usefulness is not ability but availability and trust in God's enabling power. Paul declared, "I thank Christ Jesus our Lord, who has strengthened me, because He considered me faithful, putting me into service" (1 Tim. 1:12).

This chapter also vividly illustrates what one individual, with God's help, can accomplish against the forces of evil, be they ever so firmly entrenched and powerful.

In the fourth century a monk named Telemachus wanted to live his life in pursuit of God, so he lived alone in the desert praying, fasting, and meditating. One day as he prayed, he realized his life was based on a selfish love of God, not self-less. If he were to serve God, he must serve men. He decided to return to the city where there was sin and need.

Telemachus headed for Rome. He arrived at a time when the Roman general, Stilicho, had won a great victory over the Goths. Since Rome was officially Christian, triumph brought people pouring into the churches.

But one pagan practice still lingered in "Christian" Rome—the gladiator games. While Christians were not thrown to the lions, prisoners of war were cast into the arena to fight and kill each other. Spectators roared with blood lust as the gladiators battled.

Telemachus arrived on the day of the games. Following the noise, he made his way to the arena where 80,000 people had gathered to celebrate. The fights began and Telemachus stood aghast. Men for whom Christ had died were about to kill each other to amuse a supposedly Christian populace.

Telemachus jumped the wall and in a moment stood between two gladiators. For an instant they stopped, but the crowd screamed, "Let the games go on." So they pushed the old man in monk's robes aside. Again he came between the gladiators. The crowd hurled stones at him; they urged the gladiators to kill him and get him out of the way. The commander of the games gave the order—a sword flashed and Telemachus lay dead.

Suddenly the crowd hushed silent, shocked that a holy man had been killed. The games ended abruptly that day—and were never resumed again. Telemachus, by dying, had ended them. As Historian Edward Gibbon observed, "His death was more useful to mankind than his life."[6]

FOUR

DEBORAH:
ISRAEL'S WOMAN LIBERATOR

Judges 4–5

One of the great issues of the twentieth century is the role of women in the family, the church, and society at large. Some loudly insist that the Bible discriminates against women and that the Apostle Paul is history's most outstanding example of a male chauvinist. But such unwarranted views only reveal a profound ignorance of the impact biblical Christianity has had on cultures where women have been treated as chattel, as property to be used rather than as persons to be honored. In every such case the entrance of the Gospel has elevated the status of women.

The Bible clearly affirms the equality of men and women as persons. The Scriptures also teach a difference of function for men and women, particularly in the home and the church where the man is the acknowledged leader. This does not mean the woman is inferior to the man. The Scriptures simply show how God wants the home and church to function.

There are legitimate spheres for female leadership though the matter is too rarely addressed in evangelical circles. The names Miriam, Deborah, Esther, and Priscilla remind us of women who were acknowledged leaders in biblical times. Perhaps the only one who had a major God-assigned leadership role was Deborah. She was a uniquely gifted individual and the only woman in the distinguished company of the judges. A thoughtful review of her story provides many insights.

Introduction (4:1-3)

The times in which Deborah lived and served God were dark. As long as Ehud judged Israel, the people remained faithful to Yahweh, but when Ehud died, a fresh outbreak of idolatry began. Their *rebellion* was the beginning of a new cycle that quickly brought divine *retribution* on the nation. The God who had freed Israel from the bondage of Egypt only two centuries earlier now sold them into the hands of the Canaanites.

Though the term *Canaanite* often refers to all non-Jews living west of the Jordan, the focus here is on a northern coalition of Canaanites united under Jabin, king of Hazor. Joshua had conquered and burned Hazor about 150 years earlier (Josh. 11:1-13), but the city had been rebuilt by the Canaanites and regained its previous strategic dominance over the whole region of Galilee. Another Jabin now ruled, bearing no doubt a hereditary title like the Pharaohs of Egypt. Through the brilliant help of his general, Sisera, Jabin exercised military control over six of the northern tribes, who were pushing down from Hazor, eight miles north of the Sea of Galilee, to occupy the Plain of Esdraelon, a strategic and fertile valley in the central portion of the land.

This new oppression was not brought about by a foreign invasion as the previous one had been but was instigated by the very Canaanites whom the Israelites had failed to expel from the land (Jud. 1:30-33). Israel continued to pay a bitter price for her disobedience.

Furthermore, the Canaanite oppression was a severe and extended one. For twenty years, or half a generation, Sisera, Jabin's army commander, oppressed Israel. He used Haroshethhagoyim (Harosheth of the Gentiles) as a base, a site at the western end of the Plain of Esdraelon about ten miles northwest of Megiddo.

But it was Sisera's war equipment that made the Canaanites all but invincible to the Israelites. The 900 chariots of iron were formidable and frightening weapons, enabling Sisera to control the valleys and plains of northern Israel. Gary Inrig comments,

> Their military position was nothing less than appalling. Israel was outmanned, outgunned, and out-positioned. . . . Humanly speaking, it was a hopeless situation. A nation without arms was helpless before a nation armed to the teeth.[1]

The desperate situation brought Israel to her senses. Remembering that Yahweh delights in impossible situations, they "cried to the Lord" in *repentance* and waited for deliverance. Nothing short of a miracle of divine intervention would help. And a miracle did come—in an unexpected way!

The Leadership of Deborah (4:4-9)

This section introduces us to the person who will bring *restoration* to an oppressed nation. And to the surprise of many, the leader was a lady! Deborah, as a matter of fact, is the only woman in the Bible appointed by God to be the national leader of Israel. She was an exceptional woman with outstanding leadership gifts.

She was a prophetess. As such she received revelation from God and delivered His message to the people. This message might pertain to the future or it might reveal God's will for the present. As a prophetess, Deborah joined the distinguished company of a very limited number of women in Scripture: Miriam, Moses' sister (Ex. 15:20); Huldah, a prophetess in the days of Josiah (2 Kings 22:14-20); Anna, who gave thanks in the temple for the infant Jesus (Luke 2:36-38); and the four daughters of Philip (Acts 21:8-9).

She was a homemaker. Before Deborah became a leader in Israel, she was a homemaker. Interestingly, the Bible does not say that Lappidoth was the husband of Deborah, but that Deborah was the wife of Lappidoth. Though she had a prominent position in her society, she also assumed her proper place at home as a wife and homemaker. Today's Christian career woman should seek the same balance.

She was a judge. Only one other person in the Bible was both judge and prophet—Samuel. As judge, Deborah was the political and judicial head of the nation. Holding court under a palm tree in the hills of Ephraim some eight miles north of Jerusalem, Deborah heard disputes and handed down legal decisions.

Deborah must have possessed keen spiritual insight and perspective, and in issues involving domestic affairs her decisions may have been better than a man's. The rule of a woman is not the usual biblical order, but God— unlike some believers—makes exceptions.[2]

On a coin of the Roman Empire, Judea is pictured as a captive, weeping woman seated under a palm tree. In the time of Deborah too, the nation was captive to the Canaanites and many wept because of it, wringing their hands in sorrow but taking no action. Not so the woman judge and prophetess seated under the ancient palm tree in Ephraim. Deborah was not content to accept the status quo; she was determined by God's direction to rouse the people and conquer the enemy.

She was a leader. Describing the desperate situation of her people Deborah says:

In the days of Shamgar son of Anath,
In the days of Jael, the highways were deserted,
And travelers went by roundabout ways.
The peasantry ceased, they ceased in Israel,
Until I, Deborah, arose,
Until I arose, a mother in Israel.   (Jud. 5:6-7)

The sad plight of Israel demanded a leader, and Deborah was there to fill the gap. Once assured of God's plan, she moved quickly to put it into action. Knowing she would need a sol-

dier's help, she summoned Barak from his home in Kedesh-
naphtali, a town in Galilee near the Canaanite oppressors.
Speaking as a prophetess on God's behalf, she directed Barak to
muster an army of 10,000 men at Mount Tabor in the northeastern part of the Esdraelon Plain opposite Sisera's headquarters on the western end of the plain. Deborah encouraged Barak
by declaring God's promise, "I will draw out to you Sisera . .
and I will give him into your hand" (Jud. 3:7).

For whatever reason, Barak hesitated, even in the face of
such a clear, divine command and promise, and declared he
would not go into battle unless Deborah accompanied him.
Was Barak timid and fearful? Did he lack faith? Like Moses,
Gideon, and Jeremiah, Barak was reluctant to respond to God's
call in view of the sizeable task to be accomplished. Yet the
divine call is always accompanied by divine provision, a fact
today's Christian cannot afford to forget. Paul affirmed, "Not
that we are adequate in ourselves to consider anything as coming from ourselves, but our adequacy is from God" (2 Cor. 3:5).

Deborah agreed to accompany Barak in battle but indicated
her displeasure over his attaching a condition to obeying God
by announcing that the honor of the victory would go to a
woman rather than to Barak. The statement did not refer to
Deborah but was a prophecy of Sisera's death at the hand of
Jael (Jud. 5:24-31). Thus, Barak paid a price for his reluctance
to do God's will and leaves us with a lesson to remember. God
honors prompt and unquestioning obedience to His commands.

The Military Campaign of Barak (4:10-16)

With Deborah at his side, Barak gathered an army of 10,000
men to Mount Tabor. Deborah was the only woman among this
large number of soldiers, but she was the commander in chief of
this military force. Sisera, having been informed of the Israelite
troops concentrated on Tabor, moved his massive army of chariots and foot soldiers to a temporary base at the Kishon River
some twenty miles to the west across the Plain of Esdraelon.
The disparity between the two armies is remarkable, particularly because the Israelites did not even possess shields or spears.

Thus, Barak's army had no defense against the arrows and spears that would be hurled at them, nor would they be able to throw spears at the enemy in the chariots or on foot. Hand-to-hand battle with knives and sticks appeared to be the only option. "Picture the scene then," writes John Hunter.

> In the plain we see the gathering forces of Sisera. The rattle of the chariots, the neighing of 1,000 or more horses, would present a fearsome sound to the men waiting on the hillside. The glitter of the sun on helmets, shields, and weapons, would add emphasis to remind them of their own lack of weapons.[3]

The tension of the narrative builds. Deborah gave the order to attack, and Barak with 10,000 fighting men rushed down the slopes of Mount Tabor, shouting defiance as they ran toward a powerful enemy force.

What happened next was a miracle of divine intervention. The Bible states, "And the LORD routed Sisera and all his chariots and all his army, with the edge of the sword before Barak" (4:15). The same word, translated "routed," is used in Exodus 14:24 to describe the state of the Egyptian army at the Red Sea and again in Joshua 10:10 to explain the defeat of the southern confederation of kings and their armies which had attacked Gibeon. God thus intervened on behalf of His people in the days of Moses, Joshua, and Deborah.

We learn from the song of Deborah and Barak in chapter 5 how Sisera's anticipated victory was turned into a decisive and humiliating defeat.

> The earth quaked, the heavens also dripped,
> Even the clouds dripped water. . . .
> The torrent of Kishon swept them away,
> The ancient torrent, the torrent Kishon.
> (Jud. 5:4, 21)

The scene may be reconstructed this way: as the advancing

armies approached each other, the forces of nature joined the conflict as God sent a violent thunderstorm to sweep the area. Some suggest that Deborah gave the command to attack as she saw the approaching storm, knowing that such a downpour would turn the valley into a quagmire and render the chariots useless. Whatever the sequence, the timing was providential and the defeat was complete. Sisera fled in one direction to meet his fate, and the army retreated toward their base in Harosheth-hagoyim, but none escaped. All of them perished at the hand of Barak and his brave army.

Many times I have stood on the brow of Mount Carmel at the site called El-Muhraka and relived in my imagination the stirring scenes of this great battle. The tell that is probably the site of Harosheth-hagoyim, the headquarters of Sisera, lies just off the base of Mount Carmel toward the north. The meandering stream of the Kishon River, which flows across the valley toward the Mediterranean, is plainly visible. The green and fertile plain of Esdraelon stretches some twenty miles to the east where the beautifully shaped Mount Tabor rises from the valley floor. With Bible in hand, I picture the vivid battle scenes coming to life all over again.

That God should intervene in such a miraculous manner on this and other occasions in biblical history is difficult for some to accept. A group of seminary students once sat quietly before their professor, a noted liberal in his field. The lecture was on the Hebrew exodus from Egypt. After explaining away the supernatural acts God performed to secure freedom from Pharaoh, the professor suavely described the miraculous "parting" of the Red Sea. The sea had not actually been divided, he said, but was in reality a shallow pond through which the Hebrews waded easily to safety.

"Hallelujah!" came a shout from the back of the classroom.

"What! What do you mean?" asked the disturbed professor.

"Praise the Lord!" answered a jubilant student. "I never realized what a wondrous miracle took place at the Red Sea. Imagine our Lord drowning all those Egyptian soldiers in only a few inches of water!"

The Courageous Act of Jael (4:17-23)

The story of God's intervention is not yet finished. Sisera, captain of the defeated army, fled the battlefield in a different direction from his troops. Heading north, he no doubt planned to go to Hazor to give his version of the shattering defeat of the Canaanite army to Jabin the king. Utterly exhausted, he made the fateful decision to stop short of his goal and accepted hospitality in the tent of Heber the Kenite, a nomadic group having friendly relations with the king of Hazor. (Verse 11 explains why this group, previously associated with Judah, was now living in the north.)

Jael, the wife of Heber, offered Sisera what has been called excessive hospitality, going beyond even the expectations of Near Eastern custom. No doubt she was pro-Israelite and not at all in sympathy with her husband's allegiance to Jabin. Acting with calculated efficiency, Jael concealed Sisera under a mantle and satisfied his thirst with milk or probably yogurt. Standing at the door of the tent as if to divert any curious intruders, Jael had only a few minutes to wait before the captain's deep breathing signaled that he was fast asleep. She then crept stealthily to his side and with one swift, hard blow of a mallet rendered him totally unconscious (Jud. 5:26). The mallet then came down again and again, driving a wooden tent peg through his temples, pinning his head firmly to the ground. Since Bedouin women had the responsibility of pitching the tents, Jael was adept at using a mallet on tent pegs. Sisera died instantly, and he died ignominiously at the hand of a woman (see Jud. 9:54).

When Jael saw Barak approaching in pursuit of Sisera, she motioned him to stop and showed him the corpse of the fallen leader. Barak no doubt remembered the words of Deborah, the prophetess, before the battle: "The Lord will sell Sisera into the hands of a woman."

But what are we to make of Jael's method for ridding Israel of an enemy? She has been called "the meanest of maddest murderers."

We are told her evil deed can neither be justified nor defended and that it can only be understood in the light of the ruthless times in which it occurred, times in which human life was cheap. One writer states,

> We have, however, attempted to enter into the feelings of a downtrodden, cruelly oppressed people and to understand the very human reaction of savage delight in the death of their arch-enemy and the gloating preservation of the gruesome details.[4]

Admittedly, this is not an easy matter. But we must remember that the Scriptures show the hand of God at work in these events (Jud. 4:9, 23). Jael is not condemned for her deed but is proclaimed "blessed above women" for destroying Israel's enemy (5:24, KJV). These words, as well as the "gruesome details" of the assassination, it should be noted, were penned under divine inspiration. In brief, though we are not required to admire Jael for the manner in which she carried out her mission, neither should we judge her for it. Would another means of killing Sisera have been more acceptable? Sisera was an enemy of God and of His people, a man marked for death by God Himself.

Seminary dean Walter Kaiser states, "In the case of Jael, the nation was at war. . . . Jael's loyalty to Jehovah and to His people was her justification. It was part of the old command to exterminate the Canaanite (Deut. 20:16)."[5]

The author of the Book of Judges concludes the narrative portion of his report by giving God the credit for Israel's victory over Jabin's forces and by noting that while this victory was significant, continuing pressure on Jabin had to be exerted by the Israelites until he and his kingdom were no more.

At last it is recorded that *rest* came to Israel: "And the land was undisturbed for forty years" (Jud. 5:31).

Of special significance in this chapter is the emphasis on God accomplishing His purposes through the use of human instruments. One instrument was Deborah, a strong and gifted woman who, at God's direction, set in motion the events that brought deliverance to Israel. Barak, another instrument, was hesitant and slow to respond but grew in faith and leadership and became a major force in defeating the enemy. Finally, an obscure, nomadic woman, Jael, shares honors with Deborah and Barak for bravely destroying the leader of the invading army.

Thus we see how God uses the strong and the weak, the prominent and the obscure, the gifted and the common to do His work. God uses people like Austin Gallaher, a young man whose name few people would recognize. He saved a young Abraham Lincoln from drowning in a creek. Today God is in need of people like Gallaher and Jael who, though they may be ordinary and obscure, will meet the challenge of the Lord and do what needs to be done.[6]

The Victory Song of Deborah and Barak (5:1-31)

Israel's victory over the Canaanites is recorded in prose (chap. 4) and in poetry (chap. 5). The song of victory was written by Deborah (5:7, 12) and sung by Deborah and Barak on the same day God gave Israel victory over her enemies. Likewise, Moses also sang a psalm of praise to God after the people miraculously escaped Pharaoh's army through the Red Sea (Ex. 15).

God's people should always be quick to praise Him for His mercies. While I was a seminary student, we welcomed a man from India as a member of our class. He came alone, but after some months took the bus to Boston to meet his wife as she arrived from India by boat. Many answers to prayer made this reunion possible—provision of a passport, the required visa, funds for passage, etc.

After greeting his wife warmly, the student said, "We must thank the Lord for your arrival!"

His wife replied, "Here? With all these people around?"

"Yes." So beside the gangplank, with many disembarking passengers looking on, the grateful couple fell on their knees to express praise to the Lord!

Deborah's song has been acclaimed by many as a literary masterpiece for its brilliant imagery and its vivid, dramatic style. Readers should observe that in Hebrew poetry the dominant characteristic is repetition of thought rather than sound. Accordingly, the second lines of the couplet should be examined to determine whether the thought of the first line is simply expanded or whether the antithesis is expressed.

Presented in the form of a psalm, this song seems to have been intended for use in a liturgical setting. With its great theme of God's intervention on behalf of His people, it would be sung appropriately by the tribal representatives on the occasions of their gatherings at the central sanctuary.

An introduction of praise, verses 1-5. Beginning with an exhortation to praise the Lord, these verses link the present deliverance from oppression with the past deeds of Yahweh on behalf of His people during the Exodus and wilderness periods.

The Canaanite oppression of Israel, verses 6-11. The next verses describe the dire conditions of Israel under the Canaanite yoke. The highways were deserted because they were controlled by the Canaanites. Peasants left their open villages and fled to walled cities only to find them unsafe. The Israelite army was greatly reduced in size and bereft of weapons. The reason for such pitiful conditions? Deborah declares in verse 8, "New gods were chosen." As was so often true in the Judges period, the people forgot God and turned to the gods of the heathen. For this they always paid a great price.

With the appearance of Deborah dramatic change occurred, and she called on the rich, the nobles, and the common people to sing praise to God for His deliverance.

The roll-call of the tribes, verses 12-18. Deborah and Barak are challenged to awake from apathy and initiate action. They do so by mustering the tribes for battle. Some respond, others do not. Those who came to join forces against the enemy were Ephraim, Benjamin, Machir (the branch of Manasseh that settled west of the Jordan), Zebulun, Issachar, and Naphtali. The last three are worthy of special mention because of their acts of bravery and courage.

A stern rebuke is reserved for those who put personal comfort and safety ahead of concern for their oppressed brethren. These tribes chose not to join the battle: Reuben, Gilead (including

Gad and the eastern branch of Manasseh), Dan, and Asher. Gary Inrig observes:

> There is one thing we should notice about these four and one-half tribes who did not respond to God's call. None ever again made a significant contribution to the cause of God. Asher virtually vanished except for a brief involvement with Gideon. Dan nose-dived into apostasy; the two and one-half tribes on the east of the Jordan were overrun repeatedly. . . . They lived for themselves, refusing to risk what they had, and, as a result, they lost what they had.[7]

The only two tribes not mentioned are Judah and Simeon, presumably because of their geographical remoteness. At any rate, the lesson is clear—God cherishes those who serve Him with a willing heart more than those who hold back with a reluctant spirit.

The victory over the Canaanites, verses 19-23. The allied Canaanite kings charged into the Plain of Esdraelon, expecting to reap the spoils of war, but instead they lost all they possessed. The God of Israel used the forces of nature against them. This divine intervention is illustrated by the words, "The stars fought from heaven, from their courses they fought against Sisera" (Jud. 5:20). Not even the strong war horses of the Canaanites were able to save the Canaanites, and they perished at the hands of the Israelite army. The stanza ends with a curse on Meroz, a city of Israel presumably on Sisera's escape route, for her treacherous action in refusing to help the Israelites.

The fate of Sisera, verses 24-30. In contrast to the cowardice of the people of Meroz, these verses highlight the bravery of Jael. She is lavishly praised for killing the enemy general. With a skillful use of repetition, Sisera's death is described as if in slow motion: "Between her feet he bowed, he fell, he lay; between her feet he bowed, he fell; where he bowed, there he fell dead" (v. 27).

The scene shifts to the home of Sisera where his mother

peers from her window, fretting because her son is so late in returning from battle. Her attendants assure her that as the captain he must oversee the distribution of the spoils of war. But readers know that the mother waits in vain. Her son will never return.

> The ode breaks off with effective suddenness, leaving in the reader's mind two contrasting scenes: Sisera's lifeless body at Jael's feet, and his mother with her attendants anxiously awaiting his triumphant return.[8]

The epilogue, verse 31. A brief prayer forms a fitting conclusion to this magnificent and moving poem. The prayer asks that all the enemies of the Lord perish as Sisera perished and that all who love the Lord be blessed of God.

Modern-day Deborahs

After the noise of the battle has faded from our minds, vivid impressions remain of the central character of this story. God used Deborah, the willing-hearted woman warrior, to carry out His purposes.

While not a women's liberationist, Deborah was a liberating woman. In the long annals of Hebrew history, Deborah alone stands out as the woman who led her nation out of bondage to the Canaanite oppressors. The name Deborah means "bee", and accurately describes a busy, efficient, productive woman. Furthermore, just as a bee is capable of stinging its enemy, so Deborah was God's instrument to deliver a fatal sting to the armies of Sisera.

Keeping life balanced is a difficult task. In a time of national crisis God raised up a uniquely gifted woman who successfully balanced her roles as prophetess, homemaker, judge, and leader. While few Christian woman today face such a multiplicity of divine assignments, may they all seek to balance their divinely appointed tasks as effectively as Deborah did.

FIVE

GIDEON: THE MAN CONSUMED WITH SELF-DOUBT

Judges 6

"Actions have consequences," writes the newspaper columnist as he contemplates the grim news of the week that 164 children had been afflicted with AIDS. But the New Moralists of twenty years ago, he explains, invited us to think of human action in the moral sphere as devoid of important consequences.

And so the sanctions against divorce were weakened to make sure the marriage bonds could be slipped easily whenever either partner grew bored or disillusioned. The legal obstructions to publishing pornography were for the most part knocked flat.

Sexual experience—never mind the form, never mind with whom—was pronounced Good, if not Joyful, Liberating, etc., etc.

Drug use was commended likewise for its liberating potential. Homosexuality became, as the saying goes, a lifestyle option, regardless of what Oppressive Mentalities might have said about it in the distant past (say, 1970).

Boy, oh, boy, isn't the 20th century fun? Anyway

until the bills fall due, as so many are apparently falling due today.[1]

During Gideon's time the bills were falling due as a result of the sons of Israel doing evil in God's sight. For forty years following the deliverance through Deborah, the Israelites experienced peace and freedom. But then they listened to the seductive voices of those who whispered, "Let's be truly liberated," and they returned to the lustful worship of the idols of Baal. The consequences were swift to follow as God gave Israel over to the Midianites for seven years. Again, *rebellion* brought *retribution.*

The Conditions in Israel (6:1-10)

Catastrophic conditions now prevailed in Israel as a result of the roving robber bands of Midianites. These constant invaders included not only the Midianites, but also the Amalekites, perpetual enemies of Israel, and the "sons of the east," probably the Edomites and the Ammonites. Interestingly, the Midianites were half brothers to the Hebrews, since Midian was a son of Abraham by Keturah (Gen. 25:1-6). Moses lived among the Midianites for forty years and married a daughter of Jethro, priest of Midian (Ex. 2:15–3:1). Later, Balaam became a tool in the hands of the Midianites to curse Israel (Num. 22–24). Thus, this warlike tribe from the desert, though descendants of Abraham, was filled with hatred for God's people and sought every opportunity to hurt or destroy them.

This time God used the Midianites and their allies as instruments to chastise Israel. Crossing the Jordan no doubt at Bethshan, the invaders slashed their way across the rich Plain of Esdraelon, plundering the threshed grain, the harvested crops, the flocks, and the domestic animals. Employing a "scorched earth policy," these commando attacks drained the land of its food and left the Israelite inhabitants in a state of terror and devastation.

The strategy of the Midianites was clever. They did not seek to occupy the land but simply waited until the harvest was ready. Then they swept in and overwhelmed the land, stripping it bare like a plague of locusts. A major factor in their success was a new military weapon, the camel, used here for the first time in an organized raid. These creatures possess an endurance and speed that enable them to travel as far as 100 miles a day without food or water, carrying heavy loads on their backs. No wonder the frightened Israelites were rendered helpless and were forced to leave hearth and home and flee for their lives to caves and caverns in the mountains.

The voracious appetite of the Midianites carried them across the fertile central plain to Mount Carmel where they turned south to the Plain of Sharon, another fertile area, and then drove on to Gaza near the southern border of the land. Finally, their swift animals carried the Midianites back to the desert only to repeat their wicked game at the next harvest.

It appeared that nothing could stop the Midianites. Israel was reduced to a state of national disaster. At last, coming to her senses, Israel "cried to the Lord."

God did not immediately send a deliverer to Israel as He had before. The people of Israel appeared to be turning to the Lord as a last resort, pleading for escape from their misery without giving attention to the reason for their gross misfortune; therefore, the Lord sent a prophet who probably moved about from community to community, delivering his message. The message reminded the hearers of God's work in redeeming Israel out of Egypt and rebuked them for having feared the gods of the Amorites rather than obeying the one true God of the Israelites. The people needed to recognize the nature of their sin and repent of it. Underlying the prophet's words was the message— *repentance* is necessary before *restoration*. From what follows in the text, the ministry of the prophet seems to have accomplished its purpose.

The Commission of Gideon (6:11-24)
Unique to the record of the call of this judge is the fact that the text does not simply say as before, "and God raised up a deliverer." Rather, there is an extended treatment of this judge who

was called and commissioned by none other than "the angel of the Lord." That the angel's appearance was a theophany is clear from the fact that the terms "angel of the Lord" and "the Lord" are used synonymously in the passage (6:11, 14). When the angel approached Gideon at his home in Ophrah, somewhere on the eastern side of the Esdraelon Plain, he was threshing wheat in a winepress—an act any farmer of that time normally would have considered ludicrous. It was an act of desperation because the threat of the Midianite invaders forced him to seek a secluded spot rather than the usual open and elevated place where the wind would blow away the chaff. One writer imaginatively recreates the situation:

> I don't know how long he sat under the oak watching me. That morning I was beating out my frustrations— the stick became a cudgel and the wheat represented the neighboring Midianites. The rock floor in the winepress was well-worn from years of pounding, perhaps harder than we needed to; I had huddled in this boxed-in cubicle until the years had strung into seven.
>
> Sweat poured down my beard, not from the physical exertion but from the agony of remembering that we were a people meant to be free, not to cower in caves and dens like imprisoned animals. We never knew when we would hear the stampede of camels and see our crops razed before our eyes. We couldn't lift a finger in our own defense. People can lose their crops, but the loss of self-esteem is excruciating.
>
> Then he got up from under the oak and came forward. "The LORD is with you, you mighty man of valor," he said. What blatant irony. My disheartened spirit forced a feeble reply. "If the LORD is with us, why then has all this befallen us?"
>
> His reply sent shivers down my spine, a spine once straight with vigor and strength. "Go in this might of yours and deliver Israel from the hand of Midian; do not I send you?"[2]

The dialogue between the angel of the Lord and Gideon is indeed fascinating. It surely reveals both the frailty and fearfulness of man and the love and patience of God.

● The first time the angel spoke he said, "The LORD is with you, O valiant warrior" (v. 12). At that moment Gideon could be described as a God-forsaken coward rather than as a mighty hero. But he did not yet understand that the Lord saw not only the man who was but also the man who could and would be. In the New Testament we read of an unstable man named Simon whose name was changed to Peter—the Rock. No doubt this brought chuckles from the other disciples, but the Book of Acts reveals that, by the power of the Holy Spirit, Peter lived up to his new name. And so we must remember that God does not save us and use us for what we are but for what by His grace we may become.

Gideon's response to the angel's words was to question the Lord's presence in Israel, in light of the suffering. He also questioned God's failure to provide a miraculous deliverance. How easy it is to question the presence of God because of present circumstances. But to do so is to doubt the very words of God.

● The angel spoke a second time, commissioning Gideon to go in his strength (which God would provide) to deliver Israel (v. 14). Gideon protested that he was the least qualified person for such an assignment and that he had no base for support, having come from a small, poor family.

● A third time the angel spoke, affirming the Lord's presence and power to defeat the Midianites (v. 16). But this was not enough for Gideon. He wanted a sign, some unmistakable proof that God would indeed enable him to carry out what seemed to be an impossible mission, some proof that this summons from God was authoritative. The proof came in dramatic fashion when the angel of the Lord extended his staff and touched the food Gideon had provided. In that breathtaking moment fire sprang out of the rock and consumed the meat and unleavened bread. The angel then vanished, leaving Gideon terror-stricken with the realization that he had been in the presence of God. The Lord, however, reassured Gideon who in turn built an altar and called it, "The Lord is peace" (Jud. 6:24, RSV).

Who among us when called to serve the Lord in any sphere has not like Gideon felt unworthy and unqualified? When Charles Haddon Spurgeon at nineteen was called to pastor Park Street Church in London, he was convinced a mistake had been made and the invitation was intended for another man by the same name. But understanding his strength came from the Lord he accepted and eventually became one of modern history's most influential preachers. John Haggai writes:

A few weeks before writing this, I was in Japan, the guest of a close friend and director of Haggai Institute. Unashamedly, this multinational businessman, who uses his vocation as a conduit for Christlike leadership, said, "Without Christ, I could do nothing."

You must rely on supernatural resources. This presupposes that you live in the awareness of God's presence and power. While you may feel unworthy, you must not despair. Your resources are in God, but you must exercise the faith and discipline to appropriate them.

God is calling leaders. Not power-holders. Not Madison Avenue hype artists. Not mutual congratulation experts. Not influence peddlers. Not crowd-manipulating, exhibitionistic demagogues. God is calling leaders!

Will you respond to this call in dependence on God Himself for your strength?[3]

The Preparation of Gideon (6:25-40)

Destroying the pagan altar, verses 25-32. Gideon had sought a sign from God; now God seeks a sign from Gideon. Before delivering Israel from the Midianites, Gideon was told to destroy an altar to Baal in his own community, perhaps in his own backyard. The existence of such an altar, no doubt one of many in Israel, showed the pervasiveness of idolatry in the land and graphically illumines the opening words of this chapter. No wonder God allowed Midian to perennially overwhelm Israel.

To destroy this village shrine of which his father seemed to be custodian, Gideon was told to employ a bull, the sacred animal of the fertility cult. He was also instructed to cut down the Asherah, a wooden pillar probably representing the consort of Baal. Gideon was then to construct an altar to the Lord, offer a bull as a burnt offering, and use the Asherah as firewood. Clearly, God intended this to be a judgment on the false Canaanite religion and its nonexistent gods.

Now this was no small assignment for Gideon. On several occasions I have stood on top of a Baal altar uncovered at Megiddo just a few miles to the west of Gideon's hometown of Ophrah. This altar is over twenty-five feet across and four and a half feet high, constructed of heavy stones held together by mud. No wonder Gideon needed the help of ten men to tear down an altar of such immensity and to build another altar on which an offering could be made to the Lord. The fact that Gideon carried out the task by night is probably due not so much to his timidity as to his fear of opposition and interference not only from the townspeople but also from his father's household.

Gideon's fears were well-grounded. The next morning before his father Joash was up, the angry townspeople were gathered at the door. They had already discovered the destruction of their altar to Baal. "The worshipers of Baal never neglected their morning devotions," stated a Scottish preacher. They demanded that Gideon be turned over to them for immediate execution. Apparently, Gideon was known by reputation in his community as the principal person who favored the worship of Israel's God rather than the Canaanite's Baal.

The response of Joash to his protesting neighbors is heartening. Shamed and repentant, Joash defended his son and said, "If Baal is a real god, he can contend for himself." But Gideon remained unharmed, demonstrating Baal's inability to defend himself. Baal was thus exposed as a false deity, and Gideon's new name, "Jerubbaal," meaning "let Baal plead his case" was a constant reminder of God's power and Baal's weakness.

Thus Gideon passed the test. It was not easy, but he was obedient. He knew God could not use him to deliver Israel from the Midianites until he cleaned up his own backyard. Gary Inrig pointedly expresses the spiritual implications of Gideon's assignment:

> Baal must go before Midian can go. Before Gideon could be the deliverer of Israel, he had to be the destroyer of the false god Baal. It is the same for us. Before we can have victory in our lives over the sins or problems or habits that are defeating or discouraging us, Jesus Christ must be the unquestioned Lord of our lives. There is no victory where there is idolatry or a divided heart. There can be no compromise if we desire to know the Lord at work in our lives.
>
> What is the Baal in your life? It may be any one of a hundred things. But whatever it is, it must be chopped down before God will deal with the Midian in your life.[4]

Gathering an army, verses 33-35. Trouble often follows triumph. It did for Gideon. He had won a great victory over his neighbors, but now he faced a vast army below him in the valley of Jezreel. It was the eighth annual invasion of the Midianites—and it would be their last.

To prepare God's servant for his great task of delivering Israel "the Spirit of the LORD clothed Himself with Gideon" (literal translation). This is a picturesque way of saying the Holy Spirit took complete possession of Gideon, empowering him from within. A seminary colleague tells his students, "In the morning I often pray, 'Lord, here I am. I want to be Your suit of clothes today. I want You to take me and use me. Lord, just walk around in me today.' "

Thus equipped, Gideon summoned his followers. First to respond were the Abiezrites, men of his hometown. Next came the men of Manasseh, his own tribe. Finally, troops rallied from the other tribes of the general area: Asher, Zebulun, and Naphtali. Gideon must have been encouraged by the response of 32,000 men (Jud. 7:3). But, again, fear gripped Gideon's heart. He gazed on the teeming multitudes of Midianites below him, and he shrank from the idea of leading the Israelites into battle. He needed reassurance that God wanted him to undertake this frightening task.

Confirming the will of God, verses 36-40. Gideon vacillated between faith and fear. The problem now appeared so great he may have wondered if what God had previously said (6:14-16) might be wrong. At the very least, he needed reassurance that he should proceed and that God would give him victory. The familiar test involved two steps. First, Gideon placed a fleece on the threshing floor, declaring he would be confident of victory if in the morning the fleece would be wet but the threshing floor dry. This came to pass, but Gideon was not satisfied, perhaps realizing the rock threshing floor would naturally dry before the fleece. So he asked for the reverse— that the threshing floor be wet and the fleece dry. And God patiently answered the prayer of his hesitant servant.

Did Gideon sin in asking for divine reassurance? Several points should be noted about this oft-discussed incident.

● Gideon already knew God's will. He sought another sign to confirm it.

● Gideon's faith was temporarily eclipsed by fear and doubt. Requests for signs are often described in Scripture as the product of unbelief (Matt. 12:38-39; 1 Cor. 1:22-23).

● Gideon was actually telling God what to do, i.e., what conditions had to be met before he would obey His previous orders.

● Gideon broke his promise to God by refusing to believe after the first sign and requesting a second. God's response in granting Gideon's requests does not imply approval of them but only demonstrates that He understands the frailty of human nature and treats His servants with great patience.

We must remember that after the resurrection of Christ, Thomas had doubts in his mind and insisted on a sign—that he see the nailprints and touch the scars of the crucified Lord or he would not believe. Jesus said, "Blessed are they who did not see, and yet believed" (John 20:29).

As a college student, I found myself in a position parallel to that of Gideon. Pursuing my self-chosen career in science, I was uncomfortably aware that God was nudging me toward Christian service. I was fearful of the demands of ministry but was restless and increasingly dissatisfied with my own direction. The fall of my junior year, after registering for a curriculum of advanced science courses and higher math, I confided my unhappiness to the godly dean of students. It was a crucial moment. Dr. Charles Brooks drew an imaginary straight line on his desk with a finger and then veered off suddenly in another direction. In a soft voice he said, "God wants to lead you into His will for your life, and if you earnestly want to know His direction, He will show you and not allow you to be sidetracked." He counseled that I should go to my room, open my Bible, and ask God for clear direction. It seemed so simple. I had often heard preachers talk about "putting out a fleece" to determine God's will, but I had also seen them continue on a self-determined path when the conditions were not met. For me there was no desire to dictate anything to God; I only wanted to hear His voice and know His will. Guidance came that afternoon as I prayerfully read several of Paul's epistles. Finally, one verse seemed to leap off the page, "So then do not be foolish, but understand what the will of the Lord is" (Eph. 5:17). I knew immediately that God was speaking and reminding me He had been working in my life, directing me toward the ministry, but I had been resisting out of uncertainty and fear. Now all that was required was obedience. Jesus said, "My sheep hear My voice, and I know them, and they follow Me" (John 10:27). Only two things are required to fulfill God's will: listen to His voice as you read His Word, and then follow His direction implicitly.

Gideon at last was ready to obey. Are you?

SIX

HOW TO WIN AGAINST OVERWHELMING ODDS

Judges 7–8

Hudson Taylor, pioneer missionary in China, firmly believed God knew his needs and would meet them. On one occasion, when Taylor's assets were down to 87¢, he wrote to a friend, "We have this—and all the promises of God."[1]

"God frequently cuts down on our resources," said one writer, "in order that we may depend entirely upon Him. Sometimes He sends us sickness, or financial reverses, or difficulties of one kind or another, to put us in fighting trim and train us to rely solely on His power."[2]

When God finished preparing Gideon and his army for battle, Gideon had no other choice but to trust God. The astonishing victory Gideon achieved over the enemy demonstrates that man's extremity is God's opportunity. He delights to reveal His power when men acknowledge their weaknesses. When the odds are overwhelming, God overwhelms the odds!

The Selection of Gideon's Army (7:1-8)
After Gideon's private conversations with God, he returned to his army, the 32,000 men who had responded to his summons to finally take a stand against the invading Midianites. Gideon

soon detected all was not well with the troops. Camped at the spring of Harod at the foot of Mount Gilboa, the Israelites were keenly aware of the army of Midianites numbering 135,000 (Jud. 8:10) just three or four miles north at the foot of the Hill of Moreh. Their morale was low as they now fearfully surveyed what appeared to be an impossible situation. How could an army of 32,000 untrained and unqualified soldiers hope to defeat a heavily armed force of 135,000?

How startling then were the words of God to Gideon—"Your army is too large because if I give you the victory, you will all take the credit!" It is important to see that God wanted victory in battle to teach Israel to trust Him and give Him the glory. In the Christian life if our victories make us self-reliant, they ultimately work against us and they dishonor the God we serve. Gary Inrig states:

> You cannot be too small for God to use, but you can be too big. If you want the credit for what God is doing, God will not use you. "I am the LORD, that is My name," He says. "I will not give My glory to another!" That is why, as you look around, you will see God working in a powerful way in the lives of some very weak people. They are people who are careful to give God the glory.³

The adage, "Providence is always on the side of the strongest battalion" is the opposite of the truth in Gideon's case. His army was reduced at God's command in two stages. First, in harmony with Deuteronomy 20:8, the soldiers who were "afraid and trembling" were dismissed to return home, and 22,000 hastily departed! Gideon must have watched the exodus with a sinking heart, but at least he had 10,000 men left—the number Barak had had when he won a great victory over the Canaanites. And fear could have disastrous effects on an army, so perhaps it was all for the best.

But God spoke to Gideon again, informing him that the army was still too large if the credit for the victory was to be given to the Lord. Gideon was to test the remaining 10,000 men at the nearby spring of Harod by observing how each drank. Those who bowed down on their knees to drink were to be dismissed and those who brought water up to their mouths by hand would remain. While we may regard this as simply an arbitrary test for reducing the size of the army, many feel the exercise held added significance.

Since the miracle of the victory would be greater if the battle were fought by the least qualified, it seems more in keeping with God's purpose for reducing the army to view the 300 men as those who feared a sudden ambush by the enemy and there-fore hastily scooped the water up in one hand.

At any rate, Gideon was left virtually without an army. The odds were now so preposterous that the only hope lay in God. All Gideon and the Israelites had was God's promise, "I will deliver you with the 300 men" (Jud. 7:7). Their options were limited—trust God and His promise or perish. But Gideon put his full confidence in the Lord and His promise of victory.

Gideon trusted the promise of God just as Christian and Hopeful in *Pilgrim's Progress* trusted God when caught by Giant Despair and flung into his dungeons in Doubting Castle. Their spirits were low when Christian suddenly remembered a key named "promises" in his bosom. Pulling it out, he discovered it opened every door, which led them out of Doubting Castle. As he saw the pilgrims make their escape, Giant Despair died of apoplexy.

The Confirmation of Gideon's Victory (7:9-15)

Gideon was no doubt tossing restlessly on his bedroll that night. He tried to maintain his faith by gripping God's promise of victory tightly, but in the darkness that well-known, nagging fear crept back into his heart. Then Gideon heard God's voice ordering him to attack the enemy, an action hardly fitting Gideon's mood at the time.

The Lord always understands the needs of His children. He sensed Gideon's fear and met him in his frailty by providing encouragement in a most unique way. In a remarkable demon-

stration of divine providence, He arranged for Gideon to over-
hear a significant conversation in the Midianite camp.

Picking their way cautiously down the hillside, Gideon and
his servant approached the sleeping enemy camp with hushed
breath and wary steps. They did not dare stumble and waken
some sleeping soldier or rouse some tethered animal. As they
made their way among the tents, they heard two men talking.
Gideon and his companion froze. They overheard one Midianite soldier rehearsing his strange dream: "I dreamed I saw a loaf
of barley bread roll into our camp and flatten one of our tents.
What could that mean?" The other man realized the barley loaf
represented Israel, a nation of people that had to resort to such
poor food because the Midianites had seized their wheat. The
tent could represent only the nomadic Midianites. He therefore
declared, "This is nothing less than the sword of
Gideon . . . God has given Midian and all the camp into his
hand" (Jud. 7:14).

Gideon knew at once that God had arranged it all for his
benefit—protecting the two of them as they entered enemy
territory, guiding them to one specific tent, timing their arrival
to hear the report of the dream, planting the dream in the mind
of one Midianite, and revealing its interpretation to the other.
Gideon marveled, and there in the darkness he worshiped God.
Finally, his fears were overcome, and he was prepared for battle. He was confident of victory because he finally saw how
great God is.

> God does not call us to believe in ourselves and in our
> own adequacy. Rather, He strips us bare, taking us
> down to the place where we must depend on Him.
> Then, in grace, He takes us by the hand and teaches us
> that we can trust completely in Him. We need to learn
> the lesson of dependence, so we may move on to learn
> the lesson of confidence. We learn that we can do
> nothing without Him. Then we delight to discover that
> we can rely completely upon Him. Having learned
> these great lessons, we are prepared for victory.[4]

The Defeat of Gideon's Foes (7:16–8:21)

The victory over Midian, verses 16-25. The strategic hour had arrived. Gideon carefully rehearsed with his loyal 300 the battle plan certainly revealed to him by God. First, the men were divided into three companies, a tactic often used in the ancient world (see 1 Sam. 11:11; 2 Sam. 18:2; Job 1:17). Then, the weapons were distributed—trumpets (rams' horns), pitchers (earthen jars), and torches to be hidden in the jars until the signal was given. No indication of doubt, questioning, or fear is recorded. The men were inspired by the faith and courage of their leader and, like him, were ready to trust God even though they did not understand how victory was possible against such odds and with the use of such "weapons."

Quietly, the soldiers took their positions around the Midianite camp at the beginning of the middle watch, or about 10 P.M. Suddenly, out of the darkness came the noise of 300 earthen jars smashed on the ground, the sight of 300 torches piercing the night on all sides of the camp, the sound of 300 blaring rams' horns, and the shout of 300 voices crying, "A sword for the LORD and for Gideon."

Panic seized the pagans as they imagined that each trumpeter headed a contingent of soldiers attacking from all sides.

As the sleepers stumbled out of their tents, they encountered some of their own number who had just been relieved of guard duty and imagined they were part of the enemy force that had already penetrated the camp. In the confusion, Midianite fought Midianite while the Israelites remained in their places. Thus, the enemy force broke up in wild disorder and fled toward the fords of the Jordan "trampling each other down as they raced through the darkness, and each man, as he ran, dreading to feel the enemy's sword in his back the next moment."[5] Solomon wrote, "The wicked flee when no one is pursuing, but the righteous are bold as a lion" (Prov. 28:1).

The "loaf of barley bread" had indeed flattened the tents of Midian, but the battle was the Lord's.

Pursuing the fleeing Midianites, Gideon called for reinforcements, probably from those who had recently left him, and they

joined in the chase. So did the Ephraimites, who were asked to
seal off the escape route by stopping the enemy at some of the
fords of the Jordan. The Ephraimites also slew two of the Midianite princes, Oreb ("raven") and Zeeb ("wolf"), and in accor-
dance with Near Eastern customs brought their heads to Gideon as "trophies of victory."

Once again the Lord delivered His people. He did it through
a human instrument who was hesitant and fearful, but who
finally came to trust God to work through him in his weakness.
May the Lord enable us to do the same.

Near graduation time at our seminary, I was invited to bring
an ordination message on behalf of a Chinese student who was
soon leaving Dallas to serve God in a church and seminary in
Hong Kong. Speaking through a translator, I challenged the
young man from the life of Nehemiah to be a leader. He responded by saying, "All through seminary I feared becoming a
leader. I wanted only to study and teach the Bible. Now I see
that God expects me to lead, and I will do so with His help."

The victory over tribal hostility, 8:1-21. Some sour notes
threatened to mar the astounding victory just achieved over an
enemy that had plagued the Israelites with eight successive
invasions and plunderings of the land. But Gideon diplomati-
cally and decisively handled each problem as it surfaced and
preserved the fruits of victory.

● Placating Ephraim (vv. 1-3). The powerful Ephraimites
deeply resented not being called to participate in the initial
phase of the Midianite rout, and they interrupted Gideon's
pursuit of the enemy to register their festering complaint. Their
short-tempered display of jealousy may be demonstration
enough of the validity of their exclusion.

Gideon might well have responded with emotion to the petu-
lance of the Ephraimites, but instead he soothed their feelings
with a tactful reply, commending them for the capture of the
two Midianite kings. Their contribution to the cause, in fact,
was greater than his own.

Jealousy is a hindrance to the work of God. It fosters disunity
and distracts attention from the main task of the people of

God. With his gentle answer (see Prov. 15:1) Gideon averted conflict and set a noble example for today's Christian leaders.

● Punishing Succoth and Penuel (vv. 4-9, 13-17). After the delay caused by the Ephraimite interruption, Gideon and his 300 continued to pursue of the fleeing Midianites, who had managed to escape beyond the Jordan. Israel must be fully rid of the Midianite threat. By now, however, Gideon's men were weary and hungry. Stopping at two Israelite cities on the other side of the Jordan, they asked for provisions only to be sharply refused. The leaders of Succoth and Penuel did not acknowledge what God had done through Gideon and in fact ridiculed the possibility of this ragtag army of 300 capturing the escaped kings of the Midianites, Zebah and Zalmunna. Their lack of faith in Gideon and Gideon's God meant they lived in deep fear of reprisal from the Midianites. Deeply provoked, Gideon resumed his pursuit but not before warning the men of both cities that they would experience reprisal from his hands. A man of his word, Gideon returned and punished the leaders of Succoth, beating them with thorns and briers (v. 16). He treated the men of Penuel more severely, destroying their prized tower and executing the men of the city (v. 17).

The punishment of the people of Succoth and Penuel was drastic, but their sin was serious. They refused to aid a servant of God who was carrying out a divine mission, and in the end they suffered at the hand of God for not aligning themselves with His work.

● Pursuing Zebah and Zalmunna (vv. 10-12, 18-21). Securing provisions from another source, Gideon relentlessly followed the surviving Midianite force of 15,000 to Karkor, a site thought to be located east of the Dead Sea. This is all that remained of the original Midianite army of 135,000, but it was a significant force led by two fierce kings, and Gideon with his exhausted band might have justified giving up and turning back. But Gideon was no quitter. With great tenacity of purpose he fought on, launching a surprise attack on the Midianites which resulted in the routing of their army and the capture of the two kings.

With the national crises over, Gideon was free to settle a personal account with Zebah and Zalmunna. Identifying the two kings as the ones who killed his brothers at Mount Tabor on a previous Midianite campaign, Gideon felt obligated to carry out the duty of blood revenge (Deut. 19:6, 12). When his son out of fear could not fulfill the assignment, Gideon stepped forward and slew the prisoners of war.

Persistence is a virtue in the service of God. Gideon carried out his divine calling with great constancy of purpose. When lesser men would have quit short of the ultimate goal, Gideon persisted until he vanquished the enemy and slew the last of their leaders.

A young black boy named Carver showed a similar persistence. Working his way through school, he showed promise of success in several fields. His paintings won prizes at the World's Fair Colombian Exposition. His musical genius brought him a scholarship offer to the Boston Conservatory of Music. But he chose to specialize in agricultural chemistry so he could be of greater service to his own race. He persisted for a lifetime to fulfill that goal. John Haggai records:

> Declining a prestigious teaching position at Iowa College, he packed his shabby suitcases and proceeded to Tuskegee Institute where he gave his people new goals by showing them the possibility of success. Working incredibly long hours in a shanty-type laboratory, he discovered ways to make plastics from soybeans, rubber from peanuts, flour from sweet potatoes. Thomas Edison offered him a salary in six figures. A rubber company and a chemical firm offered him blank-check retainers to work for them. But he stuck to his mission. He pursued his goals. He stayed at Tuskegee for $1,500 a year.
>
> George Washington Carver could have been a multimillionaire, but he never deviated from his goals. He has been called the 'Wizard of Farm Chemistry' and is one of the few Americans ever chosen to a fellowship

by the London Royal Society for the Encouragement of Arts, Manufactures, and Commerce.[6]

The Concluding Days of Gideon (8:22-35)

The biblical record summarizes the rest of Gideon's life with a mixture of positive and negative accounts.

The offer of kingship, verses 22-23. Gideon achieved no greater nobility than when he refused the request of the Israelites to establish a dynastic rule over the nation. He knew they were giving him credit he did not deserve when they said, "You have delivered us from the hand of Midian." Gideon was only an instrument in the hand of God, and he knew God meant Israel to be a theocracy, a people and nation ruled by God. The Israelites already had a king if only they would acknowledge Him. Their request on this occasion anticipated the fact that Abimelech, one of Gideon's sons, would later set himself up as king and that a subsequent generation would again seek a king, wanting to be like the surrounding nations (1 Sam. 8).

Gideon's spiritual insight, modesty, and humility are in sharp contrast to the events that follow.

The ephod of Gideon, verses 24-28. Although Gideon refused to be king, he did request a share of the plunder of war in the form of golden earrings stripped from their defeated foes. Arthur Cundall says:

> The man who had given such a magnificent lead to his fellows now sets a deplorable example of self-indulgence in which he, his family, and the whole nation were involved. Perhaps it is easier to honour God in some courageous action in the limelight of a time of national emergency than it is to honour Him consistently in the ordinary, everyday life, which requires a different kind of courage. Gideon, who came through the test of adversity with flying colours, was not the first nor the last to be less successful in the test of prosperity.[7]

With the large amount of gold collected, Gideon made an

ephod and placed it in his own city, perhaps on the altar he had created. There the Israelites "played the harlot" with it; in other words, they committed spiritual prostitution by having "intercourse with other deities."

The ephod was a vestment worn only by the high priest and used to discover the will of God. In Gideon's case, however, it appears to have been set up as an idol rather than being worn as a garment.

We are not told why Gideon made the ephod. Perhaps he only wanted to preserve the memory of the mighty deliverance from the Midianites by the power of God. Perhaps he did so because of the corruption of the priesthood in this period. If the theocracy were to be maintained, someone must be able to discern the will of God. But Gideon was not a Levite, and only the levitical priesthood was recognized by God. Furthermore, the only divinely approved worship center was at Shiloh, not Ophrah. Gideon made a fateful mistake by substituting his plans, however valid they seemed, for the commandments of God. It was the beginning of a sad decline in his life. In spite of Gideon's failures, however, God blessed the land with rest for a period of forty years (v. 28). Commenting on this incident, John E. Hunter warns:

> In some ways we can be like this. Great men and women can be used of the Lord. They can then start organizations, societies, or denominations, to commemorate and extend the glory of God in their work. These can function wonderfully as planned—to begin with. But then, as the vision goes, so does the response of those who follow those leaders.
>
> This can deteriorate until the purpose of the organization, society, or denomination becomes simply to maintain its own entity. So we find people dedicated to keep a certain movement in existence, regardless of whether the Lord is purposing to use it or not.
>
> Their "ephod" takes their allegiance and true effort away from the living Lord to a dead society.[8]

The family of Gideon, verses 29-31. Though Gideon refused the throne, he generally adopted a royal lifestyle. Living in considerable prosperity, he followed the pattern of the Near Eastern kings and established a large harem, which gave him seventy sons. In addition to this harem, Gideon had a concubine in Shechem, a Canaanite city, who bore him a son named Abimelech ("my father a king"). This birth set the stage for Israel's next state of apostasy.

The death of Gideon, verses 32-35. The death of Gideon apparently signaled the removal of all restraints, and the Israelites, true to form, quickly returned to Baal worship. The fickleness and faithlessness of the people is highlighted by the fact that they forgot both God and Gideon and devoted themselves to pagan gods.

In the course of his final series of Bible lectures at Dallas Seminary, Dr. H.A. Ironside said he often prayed, "O God, keep me from becoming a foolish old man!" Apparently, when Dr. M.C. Culbertson, retired president of Moody Bible Institute, heard the trustees planned to name a building in his honor, he protested, "But you don't know how I will end!"

We can thank God that—in contrast to Gideon—these men ended well. May God enable us at the end of life to say with Paul, "I have fought the good fight, I have finished the course, I have kept the faith" (2 Tim. 4:7).

SEVEN

ABIMELECH: THE RENEGADE WHO LUSTED FOR POWER

Judges 9

Over a century ago a British historian, Thomas Macaulay, made the following comment about America:

> Your republic will be fearfully plundered and laid waste by barbarians in the twentieth century, with this difference: The Huns and the Vandals who ransacked Rome were from without, and your huns and vandals will come from within your own country, and be engendered from within by your own institutions.[1]

William Penn similarly stated, "If we are not willing to be governed by God, we shall be ruled by tyrants."

In the period of the Judges, the Israelites repeatedly refused to be governed by God. In the chapter before us, the consequence of such a refusal is obvious—the people of Shechem in the center of the land were ruled by a tyrant. It was a judgment from God for their apostasy. But this time the chastisement came from within and not from without. In a future generation the Prophet Jeremiah would convey to the people of Judah these solemn words of the Lord: "Your own wickedness will correct you, and your apostasies will reprove you; know therefore and see that it is evil and bitter for you to forsake the LORD your God, and dread of Me is not in you declares the LORD God of hosts" (Jer. 2:19).

The Treachery of Abimelech (9:1-6)

The strange and tragic story of Abimelech has caused many readers of the Bible to ask why it is included in the Book of Judges. Abimelech was not a God-appointed judge of Israel. Neither did he deliver the nation from outside invaders as did the other rulers who preceded him. He was a self-appointed opportunist who had an inordinate lust for power and who committed a terrible atrocity in connection with his consuming desire to be king.

The death of Abimelech's father, Gideon, must have taken place a number of years before Abimelech came to power. The seventy sons of Gideon had grown to manhood, and even Jotham, the youngest, was old enough to make a public appeal to the citizens of Shechem.

We learn from the previous chapter that Gideon had many wives who bore him seventy sons. He also had a concubine, a secondary wife, who was the mother of Abimelech. Perhaps for this reason he experienced rejection by his brothers. Gideon, who had refused the honor of the kingship, gave his illegitimate son a name which meant "my father is king."

The story of Abimelech takes place in the central part of the country and thus portrays the spiritual condition of the Israelites in that area. It is in fact the only story in the Book of Judges which does this. The stories of Deborah and Gideon took place in the northern part of Israel, and those of Ehud and Othniel in the southeast and south. The story of Jephthah occurred east of the Jordan and the story of Samson in the southwest part of the country.

Shechem was the main city of the central region, located in a fertile valley between Mounts Ebal and Gerizim. Shechem was situated on a strategic crossroad of the route from the coastal highway in the west to the Jordan Valley in the east and the ridge route from Jerusalem in the south to the northern sites in the Jezreel Valley. It held a hallowed place in the history of Israel: Yahweh first revealed Himself there to Abraham on his arrival from Haran (Gen. 12:6-7), Jacob lived at Shechem (Gen. 33:18-20), and Joshua led the people of Israel to Shechem during the time of the conquest for a covenant renewal ceremony (Josh. 8:30-35). Though it is not stated in Scripture, apparently Shechem had been incorporated into Israel at the time of the conquest.

During the period of the Judges, the city of Shechem had a mixed population of Israelites and Canaanites, though it appears the Israelites were in control of the city. This can be implied from the fact that Abimelech asked the Shechemites whether they preferred his rule or that of his brothers. In either case the rule would have been Israelite. By giving their assent to Abimelech's kingship, the Shechemites also gave approval of his Israelite overlordship. Nonetheless, the Canaanites of Shechem strongly influenced the thinking and religious worship of the community.

Abimelech was ambitious. He had made up his mind to become king. Perhaps his lust for power was due to feelings of personal inadequacy because of his lowly birth as the son of a concubine. Whatever the reason, he was determined to make a name for himself and thus traveled the thirty miles from Ophrah, where Gideon had lived with his other wives, to Shechem where Gideon's concubine and Abimelech's mother lived with her family. It was the custom for a concubine or secondary wife to live with her own family, receiving visits from her husband only occasionally.

Approaching his mother's relatives in Shechem, he asked them to promote his campaign for kingship among the other inhabitants of the city. He intimated that seventy-one men were possible candidates for the office, but seventy of these lived at a distance. Abimelech suggested two reasons why he should be the one to become king:

1. It would be better to have one ruler than seventy;
2. He was related to the people of Shechem.

The clear implication was that Abimelech would give special attention to the local interests of the people in Shechem, a common campaign promise in every political effort. The men of Shechem may well have anticipated that Abimelech would make Shechem the national capital and that political appointments would then be made from that community.

Abimelech's campaign raises an important, contemporary question: Is it possible to be elected to high office without making improper promises or promising political favors? Referring to a person in public office, United States Senator Mark Hatfield comments:

> If he begins to sacrifice his convictions in order to accommodate himself to pressure groups for the objective of winning an election, it is like the opera *Faust*, where Faust sells his soul to Mephistopheles because he wants to accomplish certain objectives, but in the long run Faust loses. Whenever we sell our convictions for a political expediency, we never win. We have momentary victory, but in the long run we lose. In other words, I don't believe it is necessary to compromise convictions in order to win elections.[2]

Having won the support of the people of Shechem, Abimelech still faced three serious obstacles. What was he to do with the seventy other potential candidates for the office? Where would he secure campaign funds? And where would he find the support personnel to carry out the evil mission taking shape in his mind?

• The obstacle of finances was overcome by the men of Shechem donating seventy pieces of silver from the treasury of Baal-berith ("Lord of the Covenant"). The presence of this temple in Shechem shows the extent to which Baal worship existed in Israel. The account of Gideon reveals that Baal worship was prevalent in the Plain of Esdraelon, an area ruled by Canaanites until the victory of Deborah and Barak. Shechem was, however, to the south of the Esdraelon Plain in the Hill

Country less than twelve miles north of Shiloh, the home of the tabernacle. It is tragic to think there was an outpost of Baal worship in this location where Baal was called, "Lord of the Covenant," a title belonging to Yahweh as clearly demonstrated by the renewal of the covenant in Shechem in Joshua's time (Josh. 8:30-35).

● Abimelech met the obstacle of finding campaign workers by hiring "ruthless and reckless fellows" with the seventy pieces of silver given to him by the men of Shechem. These hired scoundrels were willing to do anything, even murder, for silver.

● The problem of potential competition for the kingship was overcome in a dastardly manner. Using his hired killers as a personal army, Abimelech and his men traveled to Gideon's family home in Ophrah, where he rounded up all but one of the brothers whom he intensely hated. Then they proceeded to slaughter the brothers like sacrificial animals. The implication is that this was a mass public execution. Abimelech thought he was making his ill-gotten throne secure. But Jotham, the youngest son of Gideon, escaped by hiding.

With the bloody crime completed, Abimelech and his murderous crew returned to Shechem to arrange the coronation ceremonies. Abimelech was crowned king by the average citizens of Shechem and by the noble families who lived in a section called "Beth-millo" (apparently an inner fortification or tower). His authority, however, did not extend over all Israel but only over the Shechemite territory.

The Response of Jotham (9:7-21)

Jotham, the youngest son of Gideon, was the only survivor of the bloodbath of Ophrah. Rather than running for his life, he daringly approached the edge of the city of Shechem when he heard that Abimelech had been made king. Perhaps the Shechemites were noisily celebrating in the streets of the city while Jotham climbed the slopes of Mount Gerizim. He used a rock ledge as a natural pulpit from which he denounced the shameful action of the Shechemites and urged them to reconsider their choice of king. He served as sort of a ghostly conscience delivering his "Mark Antony" speech. No doubt the citizens of Shechem were startled to hear this voice, like that of an avenging angel, and turned to listen. (It should be noted that Mount Gerizim and Mount Ebal rise on either side of Shechem, creating a natural amphitheater.)

The speech of Jotham was delivered in the form of a fable, which also turned out to be a prophecy. In fables the truth is presented in imaginary ways; animals, fish, birds, and objects, such as trees, speak, act, and think like human beings. The point of Jotham's fable is that only worthless individuals seek to lord it over others. Worthy people are too involved in useful tasks to seek such places of leadership and authority. Note that Jotham was not condemning the principle of the monarchy itself but rather was pointing out that Abimelech was a worthless person.

According to Jotham's fable or parable, the trees discussed their need for a king to rule over them and first approached the olive tree, which refused to reign since it had an important place of service to God and men. The fruit of the olive tree served as a food, and its oil was used not only to soothe the skin but also to anoint priests and kings. The trees approached the fig tree next, but it too refused the honor of kingship because its fruit was a staple food in the economy of the area. The vine also declined the exercise of authority, saying its produce—wine—was useful to both God and men. Wine was used as a libation offering to God (Num. 15:7; 28:7) and as a beverage in the homes of the people. Finally, in desperation the trees offered the kingship to the bramble. According to Arthur Cundall:

> [The bramble] not only produced nothing of value and was quite worthless as timber, but was a positive menace to the farmer who had to wage continual war against its encroachments. Its carpet-like growth was an especial menace in the heat of summer when scrub fires, fanned by the wind, could travel at incredible speeds along the tinder of dried branches.[5]

In the application of the fable, Jotham bypassed the worthless Abimelech completely and spoke directly to the men of Shechem (vv. 16-20). After describing his father's brave deeds in delivering Israel out of the hand of the Midianites, he then rebuked the Shechemites for their part in the slaughter of Gideon's sons and the elevation of Abimelech to the kingship. Jotham concluded his speech with words of biting sarcasm—wishing them well if they acted honorably and in good faith. In grimly prophetic words he predicted mutual destruction if they acted otherwise. The words of verse 20 are designated as a curse, fulfilled in the final verse of the chapter: "But if not, let fire come out from Abimelech and consume the men of Shechem and Beth-millo; and let fire come out from the men of Shechem and from Beth-millo, and consume Abimelech." One writer explains, "What is described here is total ruin—as though two enemies each firing an atomic rocket at the other in the same instant were right dead on target!"[4]

Jotham provides us with another illustration from the Book of Judges of a godly individual who acted alone but who acted courageously. Jotham had many options from which to choose. He could have reasoned that because he was alone, he would be totally ineffective, or he might have reasoned that the situation with Abimelech and Shechem was already settled and opposition would be useless. Jotham might have considered any interference foolhardy and at the risk of his life. But he didn't. He chose to stand for righteousness in an evil age and acted alone to do what he could to rebuke evil and promote justice.

The Troubled Reign of Abimelech (9:22-49)

The Discord between Shechem and Abimelech, verses 22-25. In spite of the warning of Jotham, the men of Shechem followed Abimelech for three years. The statement that Abimelech ruled "over Israel" is to be understood in a limited sense since his power did not seem to extend beyond the central areas of Ephraim and Manasseh. After three years of success, the storm began to break around him. The Shechemites no doubt disliked Abimelech making Arumah (v. 41) and not Shechem his personal residence. The Shechemites had hoped Shechem would become a prominent city after the crowning of Abimelech, but it did not come to pass. As a result, a spirit of friction developed between Abimelech and the men of Shechem. God's control of history is indicated by the fact that an evil spirit was sent to bring disharmony between the people and their petty king. This overruling action of God is also seen in 1 Samuel 16:14 and 18:10 as well as 1 Kings 22:19-23. Such passages are not to be interpreted to imply that God is responsible for sin. One author explains, "When God sends *evil* it is always an intervening force of moral and righteous judgment, corresponding to the wickedness of the situation."[5] The spirit of dissension came to a head when the men of Shechem placed armed soldiers in ambush along the trade routes near Shechem. Passing caravans were waylaid and plundered, bringing discredit to Abimelech, who could no longer guarantee safety for travelers in his territory.

The Defiance of Gaal, verses 26-29. Though Abimelech at first took no action against the marauders, the stage was set for a showdown precipitated by a new person on the scene, a wandering bandit named Gaal. He arrived in Shechem at this providential time with his brothers, and they quickly won the confidence of the fickle men of Shechem who responded to this clever demagogue as they had earlier responded to Abimelech. Shortly after Gaal's arrival was the time of the great harvest, and Gaal and his followers took that opportunity to challenge the men of Shechem to overthrow Abimelech's regime. Gaal then exhorted the Shechemites to return to an earlier allegiance: "Serve the men of Hamor the father of Shechem" (v. 28; see also Gen. 33:19). This would mean turning from Israelite rule to Canaanite rule. Finally, with great bravado Gaal challenged Abimelech to meet him in battle.

We are now able to observe a concrete illustration of the difficulties of Israelites and Canaanites living in the same community. As previously noted, both ethnic groups lived in the city of Shechem, a situation fraught with tension and temptation. A Canaanite temple of Baal-berith was in the city, and apparently the Israelites had not attempted to destroy it. In fact, the Israelites probably participated in the Baal worship at this temple. Sadly, not once in this chapter do the Israelites refer to the God of Israel. No wonder God had given explicit direction—destroy the Canaanites.

The Destruction of Shechem, verses 30-49.

● The first phase of the battle that resulted from the insurrection of Gaal is described in verses 30-41. Zebul, Abimelech's appointed ruler in Shechem, hastily and privately sent word to Abimelech that sedition was underway in the city with Gaal leading the treasonous activity. Zebul urged Abimelech to act quickly by setting an ambush against Shechem at night. Abimelech responded immediately, dividing his men into four companies, and waited for the light of day to begin the battle.

When morning dawned, Zebul and Gaal were both standing in the city gate. Gaal detected troop movements, but Zebul at first was able to allay his suspicions, saying in effect, "It is only a figment of your imagination!" When Gaal was persistent, Zebul bitingly asked him, "Where is your boasting now with which you said, 'Who is Abimelech that we should serve him?' " (v. 38) Zebul thus threw Gaal's taunt back at him and goaded him to fight. Gaal in turn—unprepared for battle though he was—was forced to fight Abimelech or lose face.

The outcome of the battle was swift. Abimelech's four companies soon defeated and dispersed the hastily gathered forces of Gaal. The further outcome of the battle was that Gaal was thoroughly discredited as a leader, and Zebul was able to oust the troublemaker and his supporters from the city of Shechem. Gaal's downfall was a direct result of his pride. Had he remained within the city of Shechem, Abimelech would have been able to do very little since the city was secure behind its walls. But he left the security of the city to act on his boastful promise to defeat Abimelech. We are reminded of Solomon's wise words in Proverbs 16:18, "Pride goes before destruction, and a haughty spirit before stumbling."

● The second phase of the battle is described in verses 42-45. Abimelech was not satisfied. He determined to teach the city of Shechem a lesson for questioning his leadership. No doubt he also wanted to make certain another Shechemite revolt would never occur. So on the next day he divided his armed men into three companies and positioned them in separate locations outside the city of Shechem. (Abimelech had learned his military strategy from his father Gideon.)

When the men of Shechem came out of the city to work in the fields, assuming the crisis was over, the signal was given and Abimelech's troops rushed the helpless workers. One company under Abimelech guarded the gate to prevent any workers from returning to the city, and the other two companies slaughtered the unarmed and defenseless people. The rest of the day Abimelech fought against the city of Shechem, killing all its inhabitants, destroying its buildings, and finally—in an act of total disdain—sowing it with salt. This procedure was a symbolic ritual, condemning the destroyed city to perpetual desolation (Deut. 29:23; Ps. 107:34; Jer. 17:6).

● The third and final phase of the battle is described in verses 46-49. When the nobles of Shechem—who were probably absent from the city at the time of the assault—heard about Shechem's destruction, they fled to the outlying tower of Shechem which adjoined the temple of Baal-berith (called here the temple of El-berith). But the Bramble Bush was blazing, and Abimelech and his men piled branches against the fortress walls and roasted alive the 1,000 occupants of the temple fortress. Thus, another Canaanite enclave was obliterated. Shechem, however, again became an important center during the days of the Israelite kingdom (1 Kings 12:1). The city was rebuilt and fortified by Jeroboam I (1 Kings 12:25). A number of years ago, newspapers ran the following story, titled "Biblical Revolution Account Confirmed":

American archaeologists have confirmed the Bible's account of a revolution which followed Abimelech's attempt to become the first king of Israel, Harvard University has announced. Evidence fixing the truth of the event was uncovered in the 4,000-year-old remains of

Shechem. . . . Abimelech's brief reign was dated at about 1150 B.C. on the basis of Shechem discoveries, Harvard reported. The archaeologists also discovered that the three buildings mentioned in the Bible [the "House of Baal-Berith," the "House of Millo," and the "Tower of Shechem"] were one and the same and that Shechem's great temple-fortress was the largest in Palestine.[6]

The Death of Abimelech (9:50-57)

Having destroyed the central city of Shechem, Abimelech now besieged and captured Thebez, a city identified by most biblical scholars with modern Tubas about ten miles northeast of She-chem. The people of Thebez probably had taken a signal from those of Shechem and also revolted against Abimelech. The inhabitants—like those of Shechem—fled to a fortress inside their city walls, and Abimelech purposed to destroy the strong-hold by fire, a method proven successful at the tower of Shechem.

This time, however, Abimelech carelessly approached too close to the walls of the tower, and he was struck down—not by a brave soldier or sharpshooter but by a woman who dropped a millstone from the roof of the tower. Some suggest the mill-stone was the type employed in a regular mill, weighing about twenty pounds, but it more probably was a handstone averaging ten to fourteen inches in length and weighing approximately five pounds. At any rate, it was a lethal weapon, and it crushed the skull of Abimelech who in his dying breath commanded his armor-bearer to spare him the disgrace of being killed by a woman (Jud. 4:9-21).

With the death of Abimelech, the vicious civil war came to an end. The men of Israel who had joined Abimelech and supported him in his campaign against the Canaanite enclave at Shechem were now leaderless and returned to their homes.

The sacred Scripture sums up the sordid tale magnificently and demonstrates that the curse of Jotham (v. 20) was fulfilled: "Thus God repaid the wickedness of Abimelech, which he had done to his father, in killing his seventy brothers. Also God returned all the wickedness of the men of Shechem on their heads, and the curse of Jotham the son of Jerubbaal came upon them" (vv. 56-57).

The final two verses explain the reason for the lengthy description of what might appear to be a less important event in the history of Israel. It was vital, especially in the period of the Judges when evil was rampant, to demonstrate for that generation and those to follow that God judges evil. A. Cohen comments, "Like a golden thread there runs through the whole scriptural narrative the doctrine that wickedness is never allowed to go unpunished."[7]

This obscure portion of Scripture contains a solemn warning for twentieth-century America. Dr. Carl F.H. Henry wrote in 1980:

> I think we are now living in the very decade when God may thunder His awesome *paradidomai* (I abandon or I give them up) (Rom. 1:24ff.) over America's professed greatness. Our massacre of a million fetuses a year; our deliberate flight from the monogomous family; our normalizing of fornication and of homosexuality and other sexual perversions; our programming of self-indulgence above social and familial concerns—all represent a quantum leap in moral deterioration, a leap more awesome than even the supposed qualitative gulf between conventional weapons and nuclear missiles. Our nation has all but tripped the worst ratings on God's Richter scale of fully-deserved moral judgment.[8]

Nearly a decade later moral conditions in our country have worsened. Can the judgment of God be far off?

A second warning from the chapter flows from the fable of Jotham. The olive tree, fig tree, and vine declined the invitation of the other trees to become king because each was "too busy," leaving the miserable bramble to assume leadership. Unfortunately, the fable accurately portrays what often happens in local, state, and national governments and particularly in the local church. Capable people who are best qualified are too often unwilling to accept responsibility and the criticism that may accompany it. A national youth organization reported an extreme shortage of people willing to serve as leaders and explained the shortfall—"there are few people who want to undergo the heat leadership positions inevitably bring." This may remind us of Matt Dillon of television's "Gunsmoke" who described his job this way: "I'm the marshall, the first man they look for and the last man they want to meet. It's a chancy job, and it makes a man watchful . . . and a little bit lonely." The Scriptures, on the other hand, challenge believers to use the spiritual gifts God has bestowed on them even when that involves the lonely task of leadership (1 Peter 4:10).

A final warning of the chapter emerges from a study of the tragic end to Abimelech's life. Paul wrote, "Do not be deceived, God is not mocked; for whatever a man sows, this he will also reap" (Gal. 6:7). Abimelech's tragic death came as a direct result of his perverted life. He reaped what he had sown. The words used to describe the career of another ruler of the Middle Ages may apply to Abimelech: "He came in like a fox, reigned like a lion, and died as a dog."

EIGHT

JEPHTHAH: THE LOSER WHO BECAME A WINNER

Judges 10–12

In 1863 Abraham Lincoln issued a document entitled, "A Proclamation Appointing a National Fast Day." Lincoln stated he believed the Civil War was a chastisement from God for the sins of the nation. He wrote:

> We have been the recipients of the choicest blessed bounties of heaven. We have been preserved these many years in peace and prosperity. We have grown in numbers, wealth, and power as no other nation has ever grown. But we have forgotten God.[1]

The next three chapters in the Book of Judges chronicle the same kind of national tragedy in Israel. In spite of all God had repeatedly done for His people, once again the Israelites forgot God.

Introduction (10:1-5)

Bridging the turbulent reign of Abimelech in Shechem and the important judgeship of Jephthah are the reigns of Tola and Jair, so-called "minor judges." Tola lived in the tribal territory of

Ephraim, adjacent to the tribe of Manasseh where Abimelech had seized power in Shechem. Since it is said Tola "arose to save Israel," we can assume he delivered the area from further strife and the spiritual deterioration which had come as a result of Abimelech's rule. After Tola's judgeship of twenty-three years, Jair judged for twenty-two years in Gilead, the Transjordanian area of Manasseh. Apparently a man of wealth and influence, no evidence indicates that he exerted a strong spiritual influence among the eastern tribes. In fact, a veritable flood of idolatry soon swept through this territory, as explained in the verses to follow.

The Rebellion of Israel (10:6)

In this cycle of apostasy, oppression, and deliverance, the sin of Israel intensified.

A sevenfold idolatry is narrated, including the Canaanite gods (the Baals and the Ashtaroth); the gods of Syria (Hadad, Baal, Mot, and Anath); the gods of Sidon (Baal and Astarte); the gods of Moab (Chemosh, etc.); the gods of the Ammonites (Molech, etc.); and the gods of the Philistines (Dagon, Baal, etc.). John Davis states, "The spiritual trends observed in Israel at this time were not merely those that reflected synchretism, but in many cases involved a total abandonment of the worship of Jehovah in favor of other national deities."[2]

The fickleness of the Israelites in light of God's treatment of them is difficult to understand. But idolatry was never simply an ancient problem. It is also a current one. With penetrating insight Donald Bloesch states,

> It is my belief that the principle challenge to the church today is the rebirth of the god of the earth, blood, and soil, a return to the ancient gods of the pre-Christian barbarian tribes. . . . This brings us again to the startling and chilling fact that the dominant issue facing the church today is idolatry. When the living God of the Bible is dethroned, other gods whom Ellul calls "new demons," will seek to take His place. The

ancient gods of the Graeco-Roman pantheon are reappearing in new guises. Mars, the god of war; Gaia, the Earth Mother; Apollo, the god of light, symmetry, and artistry. . . .[3]

Bloesch narrows his comments to the American scene. America's first strategic missile, developed in the late 1950s, was called Jupiter, the Roman god associated with lightning and thunder. Nuclear submarines have been given such names as Poseidon, the Greek god of the sea, and Trident, Poseidon's three-pronged spear. These are signs that current militarism is a religious and not simply a political phenomenon.

Still another nuclear submarine has been christened Corpus Christi [Body of Christ], dramatically symbolizing the final blasphemy against the living God. The gods of nation, race, class, military valor, nature, technique, sex—these and many others are competing to fill a void that has been spawned by an antireligious secularism.[4]

Israel soon discovered the sin of idolatry promised a great deal but delivered little. It promised freedom, pleasure, and prosperity, but delivered bondage, guilt, shame, and death.

The Retribution of Yahweh (10:7-9)
The apostasy of Israel aroused the anger of the Lord: "And the anger of the LORD was hot against Israel" (v. 7, KJV).

To chastise His people the Lord turned them over to their enemies, the Philistines in the west (anticipating the Samson story in 13:1–16:31) and the Ammonites on the east side of the Jordan River. Reuben, Gad, and the half tribe of Manasseh had settled in Trans-Jordan, and now they suffered at the hands of fierce Ammonite armies that repeatedly devastated their lands. But the tribes of Judah, Ephraim, and Benjamin were not spared as their armies encountered the awesome power of Ammon spreading into the central hill country of Israel. The severe character of the suffering is reflected in the terms *afflicted* (literally *shattered)* and *crushed* (v. 8).

The Repentance of Israel (10:10-18)

After eighteen long years, "They suddenly realized that idolatry had betrayed them and that heathen idols were entirely impotent to help them in the time of crisis."[5]

The repentance of the nation is recorded in two stages.

● In the first stage the sons of Israel acknowledged their sin in specific terms: "We have forsaken our God and served the Baals" (v. 10). John Hunter declares,

> With our educated hindsight it is easy to look at these people and condemn them. How stupid they were! They never seemed to learn! They only had to recall what had happened before to realize they were deliberately walking into trouble, but nothing stopped them! This is the way the Holy Spirit wants us to react. He wants us to recognize their utter foolishness, not just to condemn them. When we look at them, we are really looking at ourselves. In so many ways our lives are reflections of their rebellion. And the reason is simple—we have no King, and we are doing what is right in our own eyes.[6]

To Israel's initial indication of repentance, the Lord responded by rehearsing the history of His faithfulness in delivering the Israelites from their enemies. He delivered them from Egypt (Ex. 14); from the Amorites (Num. 21); from the Ammonites (Jud. 3); from the Philistines (Jud. 3:31); from the Sidonians (no specific reference); from the Amalekites (Ex. 17 and Jud. 3); and from the Maonites (perhaps a reference to the Midianites as per the Septuagint).

The chilling words, "Go and cry out to the gods which you have chosen; let them deliver you in the time of your distress" (v. 14), pierced the hearts of the backsliding Israelites. John Hunter says:

Do not miss the thrust of these words. The gods they served provided opportunities for sin, but there was no salvation from their hands. It is the same in our day. Many people are seeking and following the gods of lust and pleasure and materialism. They too provide many opportunities for excitement and blatant sinfulness, but they cannot save a precious soul.[7]

● The second stage of Israel's repentance is now demonstrated in four ways. First, the Israelites confessed their sins to the Lord (v. 15a). Second, they bared their backs for punishment (v. 15b). Third, they put away the idols representing foreign gods (v. 16a). And fourth, they served the Lord (v. 16b).

The Israelites had demonstrated not only by words but also by actions their sincere repentance, and God responded. In fact, nowhere is the grace and mercy of God and His intense love for Israel more clearly revealed than in this situation. The inspired record declares, "He could bear the misery of Israel no longer" (v. 16c). Adam Clarke writes,

> What a proof of the philanthropy of God! Here His compassion moved on a small scale, but it was the same principle that led Him to give His Son Jesus Christ to be a sacrifice for the sins of the whole world. God grieves for the miseries to which His creatures are reduced by their own sins.[8]

In the providence of God everything then came to a head. The Ammonites regrouped their forces for battle, and Israel assembled at Mizpah (probably a reference to Ramath-mizpeh, a location fourteen miles northeast of Rabbath-ammon). War was obviously imminent, and Israel apparently had no qualified military leaders.

The Restoration of Israel (11:1-40)
Jephthah's Call to Leadership, verses 1-11. The desperately needed leader to bring deliverance from the Ammonite scourge now

appeared on the scene, and his name was Jephthah. Jephthah was a man with a strange background. In fact, many would say he was a "loser." He was an illegitimate son, having been born of a harlot. He was resented by his half-brothers and eventually driven out of his home. Fleeing to the land of Nob, a frontier region to the north of Gilead, he gathered a small band of men about him and became their leader. Arthur Cundall reminds us:

> There is some correspondence with the factors that shaped the career of David who, driven into the wilderness by Saul's jealousy, gathered to himself those who were in distress or in debt, or who were discontented (1 Sam. 22:2), and welded them into a formidable force. At a later stage, still pursued by Saul and unsure of the loyalty of his own countrymen, David went over to the Philistines as a mercenary captain, learning the arts of warfare which were to serve him in good stead in the course of his long reign.[9]

It seems improper—in view of what we later learn about Jephthah's character—to ascribe to him and his men lawless activity such as ruthless pillaging of villages. More than likely, Jephthah, like David, protected settlements from marauders. Thus Jephthah acquired the skills of a fighter and established a reputation as a military leader. From what then transpires, we can surely see the providence of God working in the life of this man, preparing him for the leadership of His people against the Ammonites.

When the anticipated attack from the Ammonites came to pass, the elders of Gilead were desperate to find a military leader. So they journeyed to Tob to search out Jephthah and to seek his help.

Jephthah's experience was not unlike that of Winston Churchill. The British leader had been politically ostracized prior to World War II because of his unpopular warnings against Nazi Germany's militarism, but after the disaster at Dunkirk in 1940, the British sent for Churchill, and he was made Prime

Minister.[10]

When the elders proposed to Jephthah that he be their military leader in the struggle with the Ammonites, Jephthah countered by insisting he would only accept their offer if he would be acknowledged as their leader after as well as during the Ammonite war. "If victory is achieved over the Ammonites," Jephthah said to the elders, "it will only be because 'the LORD gives them up to me' " (v. 9). The elders quickly agreed to the demand of Jephthah, and the agreement was sealed in a solemn ceremony in Mizpah. At the inauguration or coronation ceremony "Jephthah spoke all his words before the LORD at Mizpah" (v. 11).

It seems clear that Jephthah's experience in the wilderness as an outcast from his family brought him into a close walk with the Lord God. The same was true in the lives of Moses, David, Elijah, and the Apostle Paul. Our own wilderness experiences or times of affliction often have the same effect. They reduce us to the place where we can only look to God for His direction and deliverance.

Jephthah's Military Strategy, verses 12-29, 32-33. No doubt everyone expected Jephthah to launch an immediate military attack on the enemy, but he did not do so. Instead, he attempted a negotiated settlement with the king of Ammon, asking the king why he was coming against the Israelites. The reply came back that it was because Israel had seized Ammonite territory at the time of the Exodus and conquest. The demand of the king was simple—restore their lands immediately!

Jephthah replied lucidly by tracing Israel's history, defending Israel's right to territory in Trans-Jordan. Jephthah countered the king's charge with four arguments.

• First, Jephthah argued that Israel had not taken the land from the Ammonites but from Sihon, king of the Amorites (vv. 15-22). Since the Israelites took the land from Sihon the Amorite in battle, they had a legitimate claim to this territory.

• Second, Jephthah argued that since the God of Israel gave His people the land in question, they had the right to possess it. He went on to say that even the Ammonites surely recognized that victory given by a deity entitled the victors to the conquered territory (vv. 23-24). The mention of Chemosh in verse 24 is perplexing since Chemosh was the god of the Moabites; however, Jephthah was familiar with the history and culture of the lands east of the Jordan and knew that at least for a period of time the Ammonites worshiped not only Malcam (or Molech) but also Chemosh. Of course, Jephthah is not acknowledging the reality of the false god Chemosh. He is speaking ironically and may be implying that because the God of Israel had done more for His people than Chemosh had been able to do, Yahweh possessed the superior power.

● Jephthah next argued from the matter of political precedent by reminding the king of Ammon that Balak, the king of Moab, did not dispute Israel's right to the Moabite territory, which Israel had taken when she defeated Sihon, king of the Amorites (Num. 21:26). This constituted tacit acknowledgment of Israel's right to retain conquered territories (Jud. 11:25).

● Finally, Jephthah argued that the "statute of limitations" had expired since Israel had now held this territory for 300 years (v. 26). It was too late for Ammon to press her claim since Israel had enjoyed such a long period of undefeated occupation of this region.

The reference to the Israelite possession of the land in question for 300 years is significant. Since Jephthah's judgeship began about 1100 B.C., adding the 300 years mentioned here dates the conquest at approximately 1400 B.C. The Exodus forty years earlier took place, therefore, around 1440 B.C., the "early date" held by most evangelical scholars.

Jephthah's efforts went for naught. His cogent arguments fell on deaf ears, and he therefore had no alternative but to fight. But Jephthah was not left to grapple with the enemy in his own strength: "The Spirit of the LORD came upon Jephthah" (v. 29). When God calls a man to serve Him, He always enables him for the task. The Apostle Paul, another man with an undesirable background, thanked the Lord for enabling him in his ministry: "I thank Christ Jesus our Lord, who has strengthened me, because He considered me faithful, putting me into service; even though I was formerly a blasphemer and a persecutor and a violent aggressor. And yet I was shown mercy, because I acted ignorantly in unbelief; and the grace of our Lord was more than abundant, with the faith and love which are found in Christ Jesus" (1 Tim. 1:12-14).

With an army no doubt much smaller than the enemy's army, Jephthah courageously engaged the enemy in battle and "the LORD gave them into his hand" (Jud. 11:32). It was a remarkable and decisive victory, which delivered Israel from her enemy of eighteen years.

Jephthah's Vow to the Lord, verses 30-31, 34-40. Before the crucial battle, Jephthah spent some time with the Lord. He earnestly desired victory and realized that he could not achieve it apart from God's help. In keeping with Old Testament practice Jephthah made a vow to the Lord. While it appeared to be an act of deep piety, some feel the vow was rash and tragic. Scholars differ widely as to what Jephthah meant by his vow and the manner in which he carried it out.

● A view held by many is that Jephthah thought a human being would come out of his house to greet him; therefore he deliberately anticipated offering a human sacrifice to win God's favor and grant him victory. According to this view, he carried out the vow by slaughtering his daughter and offering her body as a burnt offering.

● A second view also widely held is that Jephthah expected either an animal or human being to come out of his house and meet him when he returned from battle. If an animal came out, it would be sacrificed as a burnt offering; if a person appeared, he or she would be dedicated to Jehovah for lifelong service at the tabernacle. This view is reflected in the NASB translation of verse 31: "Then it shall be that whatever comes out of the doors of my house to meet me when I return in peace from the sons of Ammon, it shall be the LORD's, and I will offer it up as a burnt offering." According to this view, Jephthah's daughter remained a perpetual virgin and served the Lord during her lifetime at the tabernacle.

● A third view is that Jephthah expected a person would meet him. In carrying out the vow then, he did not slaughter his daughter but made her the Lord's in another sense. The following arguments support the third view:

1. It seems clear that the object of the vow was a person (see Josh. 2:19 for the same grammatical construction). It is extremely doubtful the conjunction should be translated "or," giving Jephthah the option of offering a person to lifelong religious service or an animal as a burnt offering. The second phrase is in apposition to the first as reflected in the *Authorized (King James) Version* and the *New International Version.*

2. It is best to understand the clause, "It shall be the LORD's" in terms of what Hannah meant when she said of her unborn child, "I will give him to the LORD all the days of his life" (1 Sam. 1:11). As the text reveals, Hannah gave up Samuel for temple service under Eli the priest.

3. Several Old Testament passages indicate there were orders of unmarried female servants at the tabernacle (cf. Ex. 38:8 and 1 Sam. 2:22). Possibly the story of the daughters of Shiloh in Judges 21 refers to a group of young ladies who were tabernacle servants in the pattern intended for Jephthah's daughter. Clearly, they were unmarried women because they were available as potential wives for the Benjamites.

4. The Hebrew word for burnt offering does not connote the idea of death but speaks only of something being offered up to God completely. This was carried out in animal sacrifice but also would have perfectly described a young woman giving herself completely to the Lord as a temple servant.

5. The text emphasizes the perpetual virginity of Jephthah's daughter (vv. 37-39). The young woman and her companions wept because of this, and the result was that, "She had no relations with a man" (v. 39). The grief expressed by Jephthah, his daughter, and her companions was appropriate because she was an only child and her perpetual virginity meant this family would have no progeny, a special misfortune to any Jew (Lev. 20:2; Ps. 78:63). Jephthah mourned the termination of his lineage.

6. Jephthah is cited approvingly in Samuel's address to the nation (1 Sam. 12:11), and in Hebrews 11 he is listed beside Samuel and David.

7. Human sacrifice was contrary to the Mosaic Law (Lev. 18:21; 20:2-5; Deut. 12:31; 18:10) and Israelite practice. How can we suggest that God-fearing Jephthah could have supposed it would please the Lord to practice what was an abomination to the God of Israel? No Jewish priest would have submitted himself to this human rite nor would the people of Israel have tolerated it. When a foreign king offered his son as a human sacrifice, the Israelites became very angry and promptly left the area (2 Kings 3:27).

8. On careful examination the text does not support the idea that Jephthah made a rash vow. His emotional balance and logical outlook on life are clearly demonstrated by the fact that he sought to negotiate peace with the Ammonite king rather than rush rashly into war. The vow was made by one who had a high respect for God and His will.

9. The passage makes no claim that human sacrifice was involved in carrying out Jephthah's vow. It only states, "He did to her according to the vow which he had made" (v. 39). The words immediately following, "and she had no relations with a man" seem to define the manner in which the vow became effective for the young woman, namely by committing her to a life of continual celibacy.

10. Finally, we note that the Spirit of the Lord came on Jephthah to enable him to win a remarkable victory over the Ammonites. It is extremely difficult to believe God would have granted the victory if Jephthah's vow intended the sacrifice of a human being.[11]

We must not leave this passage simply with a collection of arguments favoring any particular point of view. We should be challenged and motivated by these biblical characters, a father and his daughter, who were obedient to what the Scriptures taught regarding the requirements of God in respect to the payment of vows (Jud. 11:36-39; Num. 30:2; Deut. 23:23). As New Testament Christians we are not under the Old Testament

law of vows; nonetheless we too should be faithful to any prom
ises and commitments we have made to the Lord.

> In the Church are a multitude of spiritual failures—
> Christians who have covenanted with God to serve
> Him in one way or another but have not had the fideli-
> ty which Jephthah showed. They have agreed to teach
> Sunday school classes, but after halfhearted efforts have
> given up, "too busy" to invest time in training, in les-
> son preparation, or in visiting with and praying for
> their children or adults. They have accepted offices in
> the church, or membership on committees, but have
> neatly sidestepped each assignment and "let George do
> it."
> The Lord wants men and women who will regard the
> acceptance of a church responsibility as a solemn obli-
> gation, and not take an office or position when they
> have no intention of discharging the responsibilities
> that go with it.[12]

Epilogue (12:1-15)

The War with Ephraim, verses 1-7. The tribe of Ephraim aspired
to lead and apparently had an attitude of superiority with respect to the other tribes. If its influence was ignored or its
superiority not recognized, the tribe of Ephraim was easily of-
fended. The Ephraimites had been angered on a previous occasion when Gideon did not invite them to participate in his
surprise attack on the Midianites (Jud. 8:1-3). Now, jealous of
Jephthah's victory over the Ammonites, they crossed the Jordan and expressed their resentment to Jephthah in cruel and
scornful words. Once again they accused the military leader of
failing to summon them to war against the common enemy and
threatened Jephthah's life saying, "We will burn your house
down on you" (v. 1).

Jephthah responded to their insulting words with quiet courage and great determination. His approach was much more
confrontational than Gideon's approach of placating the Ephra-

imites with soothing words. Jephthah affirmed he had indeed summoned the Ephraimites, but they had failed to respond. As a result he said, "I took my life in my hands" (v. 3) and attacked the Ammonites with a small force. He pointed out that it was the Lord who gave him the victory.

The Ephraimites were not satisfied. They provoked the Israelites with a sneering aspersion that Jephthah's soldiers, the Gileadites, were renegades; that is, they were refugees or deserters from the tribes of Ephraim and Manasseh on the west bank of the Jordan. The deep-seated feelings of hatred between the tribes produced a tragic civil war. The battle, however, was short and decisive as the army of Jephthah, hastily recalled, won a complete victory over their countrymen. This intertribal war spelled disaster for the tribe of Ephraim, which did not fully recover and achieve recognition and leadership until after the downfall of Solomon.

Following the battle, Jephthah and his men captured the fjords of the Jordan, intending to prevent the surviving Ephraimites from returning to their home west of the river. Any who attempted to escape across the Jordan were challenged to identify themselves by repeating the word *Shibboleth* ("ear of corn"). This password contained a consonant the Ephraimites were incapable of pronouncing. As a result, Jephthah and his men slew 42,000 on the spot. The Ephraimites were betrayed by their speech as was Peter in the courtyard of Caiaphas' palace (Matt. 26:73).

During the American Civil War soldiers from "border states" spoke very much alike whether they fought on the side of the Union or the Confederacy. Consequently, it was easier for spies from these areas to work undetected behind the lines in enemy territory. Conversely, soldiers from far northern or southern states had a more pronounced accent and were betrayed by their speech. Likewise, during World War II, Nazi spies who learned English in the German classroom were often exposed when they were asked to say English words that a German-speaking person finds difficult to pronounce.[13]

With respect to the Ephraimites, it should be noted that the tongue kindled the flame (v. 1) and the tongue betrayed them (v. 6). Tragically, many times since this sad event, strife among the people of God has occurred because of the same sort of pride, jealousy, and hurt feelings.

While it appears to us that Jephthah's retaliation was excessive, he apparently continued as a respected leader east of the Jordan. He served that portion of Israel as a judge for six years.

The Successors to Jephthah, verses 8-15. Jephthah was followed by three minor judges. Little is said concerning these men and the events during the twenty-five years they served, but it is apparent they were instrumental in keeping peace in the land.

• Ibzan (vv. 8-10) is mentioned only here in the Old Testament. His home was in Bethlehem, probably the Bethlehem located in Zebulun, about ten miles north of Megiddo (Josh. 19:15). The size of his family would indicate he was a polygamist, who sought to increase his sphere by establishing marriage relationships with families throughout the land of Israel.

• Elon (vv. 11-12) was also from the tribe of Zebulun. Nothing further is stated concerning this judge except the length of his period of office (ten years) and the place of his burial.

• Abdon (vv. 13-15) was from a town in the territory of Ephraim. The fact that he had forty sons would indicate he too was a polygamist. As noted, his thirty grandsons "rode on seventy donkeys," a mark of prestige and prosperity. Abdon was buried in his hometown in the land of Ephraim, a portion of what at that time was apparently occupied by the Amalekites.

Thus concludes the story of Jephthah and his immediate successors. The lessons from this section of the Word of God are many. We cannot help but be impressed with God's patience and compassion for His sinful people. The power of God is visible in His ability to deliver His people, and His grace is demonstrated in His use of weak and frail men as His instruments. He still delivers His people and demonstrates His grace. It has often been said God does not save us and use us because of who or what we are but because of what we may become. As for Jephthah, John Hunter comments,

There he is (in Heb. 11), the illegitimate nobody from nowhere, next door to David and Samuel. And all because in his life there was a King to whom he sought to give honor and glory and obedience, and before whom he set out to do what was right in His eyes, and to whom he gave all that he possessed—his only child.[14]

Jephthah may have been an ordinary man, but he accomplished some extraordinary things. Likewise, the 1988 Winter Olympics brought to public attention a non-hero from Great Britain named Eddie "the Eagle" Edwards. Eddie is nearly blind but has a deep desire to be a ski jumper. Though he finished last in the event, he became a national hero, sought out by crowds who wanted his autograph or desired to interview him. He is an ordinary person who attempted something unusual and succeeded.

We too may sense our ordinariness, yet if we set our eyes on the goal of accomplishing something for God, and if we trust Him for enablement, we too can rise above the ordinary and accomplish something extraordinary for the glory of God.

NINE

SAMSON:
THE JUDGE WHO
WAS PHYSICALLY STRONG
AND MORALLY WEAK

Judges 13–14

The story of Samson is one of the strangest in the Bible—at once the story of a great opportunity and a dismal failure. The puzzle of Samson's life is this: while he was so richly endowed with potential for blessing and victory, he failed to live up to his potential and ended his life in disgrace. Lay leader Robert Foster writes:

> In raw, giant strength and wild daring Samson stands alone. He was a man of wit but not of wisdom; he was great but could have been outstanding. As with so many men . . . his strength was his weakness. Along with his physical strength was moral weakness; there was strictness . . . yet laxity. Many a man like Samson has loved some woman "in the valley of Sorek." The entire world is a valley of Sorek to weak men and at every turn, he needs someone higher than himself to guard and guide him. Like this Judge of Israel, his unbridled passion and overwhelming desires made him a child in morals, though full grown in mind and muscles.[1]

Samson was to be a leader in Israel, was to be God's instrument to deliver His people, but unfortunately his walk with God was erratic and his contacts with God infrequent.

Sir Thomas Beecham was once leading a rehearsal at Carnegie Hall as guest conductor of the New York Philharmonic. His glance fell on an inattentive second violinist gazing at the ceiling and scraping his bow out of harmony with the rest of the players. Sir Thomas urbanely continued to the end of the movement and then remarked to the offender, "We cannot expect you to follow us all the time, but would you have the kindness to keep in touch with us occasionally?"[2]

Perhaps God felt the same way about Samson. He probably feels this way about us, when He looks our way and finds us inattentive to Him and insensitive to His desire for daily contact and fellowship.

Because Samson's feats of strength are so unusual, many liberal scholars suggest the story of Samson is but a Hebrew version of the legend of the Greek strongman Hercules. Dr. Gary G. Cohen explores the supposed connection between the feats of Samson and the labors of Hercules in a scholarly article in *The Evangelical Quarterly*. Dr. Cohen concludes there is "no basis for the rationalistic assertion that Hercules provides the pattern for the Samson narrative."[3]

Even though the story of Samson is difficult to understand and evaluate, it cannot be ignored nor even minimized. The extent of the report of this judge in the Book of Judges is remarkable. Nearly one fifth of the book is about Samson, a fact which should remind us that he played an important role in Israel. In addition, the story of his life has provided helpful guidelines for God's people through the ages.

The Rebellion of Israel (13:1a)

The dreary pattern once again repeats itself. "Now the sons of Israel again did evil in the sight of the LORD." Nothing thus far in the dreary history of the period of the Judges restrained Israel from the seventh recorded apostasy (3:5-7, 12-14; 4:1-3; 6:1-2; 8:33-35; 10:6-9). Apparently the apostasy mentioned here was part of the total abandonment of the worship of Yahweh recorded in Judges 10:6, where we are told the Israelites gave themselves over to a sevenfold idolatry, including the worship of the gods of the Philistines. Sadly, each new generation must learn the lessons of the price to be paid for sinful indulgence.

The Retribution of Yahweh (13:1-6)

As punishment for their idolatry, the Lord allowed the Philistines to oppress Israel forty years—the longest recorded oppression Israel experienced. The career of Samson is set in this time.

The Philistines, forced out of their homeland in Greece and the Aegean Sea, attacked Egypt around 1200 B.C. Defeated, they moved north and settled on the coastal plain of Palestine, where they organized a pentapolis, or confederation, of five cities—Gaza, Ashkelon, and Ashdod on the coastal highway; Gath and Ekron on the edge of the foothills of Judea. An earlier reference is made to the Philistines in the time of Shamgar (Jud. 3:31), but now they become Israel's fierce and foreboding enemy. In fact, the forty-year period of oppression was not to end until the Battle of Mizpah (1 Sam. 7:7-13) when Samuel would lead the Israelites to a victory over their Philistine foes. During the reign of King Saul, the Philistines would reassert their power and penetrate as far inland as Bethshan (1 Sam. 31:10). The Philistines would not be finally defeated until the early years of David's reign (2 Sam. 5:17-25).

A close examination of the passage before us reveals a sad and solemn omission. At every other point in the story of the judges, the Israelites reached a time of desperation, then they repented and cried out to God for a deliverer (3:9, 15; 4:3; 6:7; 10:10). But that did not happen in this case. The people were apparently unaware of the danger they were in and were enjoying the time of national affluence. The rule of the Philistines at this time was not cruel and onerous, and the Israelites not only accepted their rule with apathy and docility but even came to resent Samson's exploits to deliver them (Jud. 15:11). The Lord therefore did not send a national deliverer but instead raised up

Samson, who waged a one-man war against the Philistines. He recognized the danger of compromise with the enemy, foreseeing that Israel could lose her national identity. We must judge Samson harshly because despite his privileges and his calling, his life revolved around self-indulgence. We are left wondering what he might have achieved, though we recognize his contribution to the preservation of his nation in a very crucial and dangerous period.

The Restoration of Israel (13:2–14:20)

The parents of Samson, 13:3-23. Samson's parents lived in Zorah, a town located on the border between Dan and Judah. The town was opposite the town of Beth-shemesh on the northern side of Sorek valley. Samson came from an area that had known the oppression of the Philistines.

Like Sarah and Elizabeth, the wife of Manoah was barren and childless. Her condition was considered a tragedy in Israel because the family line could not be continued. Her intense frustration, however, was put to an end by two appearances of the angel of the Lord.

● The wife of Manoah may have been at work in the fields one day when the angel of the Lord, a theophany, appeared to her, bringing an astounding message to this Danite woman—an answer to her deep longings and prolonged prayers. The visitor said, "Behold, you shall conceive and give birth to a son, and no razor shall come upon his head, for the boy shall be a Nazirite to God from the womb; and he shall begin to deliver Israel from the hands of the Philistines" (v. 5).

Scarcely believing what she had seen and heard, the woman ran across the fields to breathlessly relate to her husband the message she had received from the angel.

Central to the announcement of the angel was that the son would be a Nazirite, one obligated to keep the law of the Nazirite vow (Num. 6:1-8). The Nazirite vow was undertaken by a man or a woman voluntarily and for a limited period of time in order to fulfill some special service to Yahweh. The word *Nazirite* means separated or consecrated. The heavenly messenger instructed that the child was to demonstrate his separation to the Lord by keeping the three requirements of the Nazirite vow:

1. He was to abstain from the fruit of the vine, indicating his dedication to live a simple life;

2. He was to refrain from cutting his hair as a public sign of his vow to God;

3. He was to avoid contact with a dead body, an act that would disqualify him for tabernacle worship.

Samson was to avoid anything that marred his fellowship with God. Clearly, these outward actions would be meaningless unless they truly represented an inner dedication of life.

The angel made it clear that Samson was to be a Nazirite all his life; that is, "from the womb to the day of his death" he was to be a man marked by dedication to Yahweh. Even his mother was required to refrain from drinking strong drink or eating unclean foods while she was carrying the child lest he be contaminated with that which would violate the Nazirite vow.

But what was in the mind of God when He imposed this lifelong requirement on Samson? Leon Wood comments:

> Samson was to be highly honored by entrustment with a continual miracle of life. He would be endowed with greater physical strength than any other man. To put it so, he would be a living miracle all the time he lived. This meant that God was extending to Samson a high privilege, but at the same time a heavy responsibility. He would have the responsibility to refuse the temptation to use this strength for his own honor or to further selfish ends; he would have to remain humble and recognize that his unique gift was to be used only for the glory of God. Then Samson would have to live such a life of dedication that others, both Israelites and Philistines, would be able to see evidence that he was truly devoted to God, and that they might appropriately recognize the true source of his strength. The credit and honor for it should not go to Samson, but to God.

Samson was responsible also for reminding himself continually that his strength was really not his own, but it was God's entrustment to him and that he had to continue to live properly before God if this entrustment was to continue. The outward actions of the Nazirite form of life were suited exactly to helping Samson dispose of these responsibilities. They provided a daily and continual reminder so that he would not forget as long as he adhered to them.⁴

The angel also revealed that in addition to being set apart as a Nazirite, Samson had an extremely important role to play: "He shall begin to deliver Israel from the hands of the Philistines" (v. 5). The completion of the great task of delivering Israel from the Philistines would be left to others such as Samuel, Saul, Jonathan, and David. The yoke of the Philistines would not be broken in Samson's time because Israel would not repent. But God did not abandon Israel. He raised up Samson to begin the work of liberation.

● The second appearance of the angel came in answer to the prayer of Manoah (vv. 8-20). Strikingly, Manoah did not dismiss his wife's report of the angel's appearance as an imaginary or emotional event, but he immediately asked the Lord to send "the man of God" again that "he may teach us what to do for the boy who is to be born" (v. 8). The angel did reappear, and Manoah asked a second question, "What shall be the boy's mode of life and his vocation?" (v. 12) The angel did not respond to the question but cautioned Manoah's wife to be careful to observe all the restrictions he had previously imposed. Probably Manoah was too inquisitive as to what sort of son the child would be. He should have been content with what God had revealed. Leon Wood explains:

In this display of curiosity, however, Manoah was much like God's people of any day. The desire is to know all steps ahead in a course of action God has ordered, before beginning with the first step then trusting God to reveal the others in their proper time. God wanted Manoah to be content and trust Him for succeeding matters pertaining to this son.[5]

We must note that Manoah and his wife desperately wanted to fulfill their parental responsibility and raise their child to honor and serve God. That is why Manoah was initially motivated to ask, "How shall we bring him up?" All evidence seems to indicate that this husband and wife were concerned about doing their best as godly parents for Samson. Why then was Samson's life and career so checkered? The answer can only be that Samson continually made wrong choices. To raise a dedicated and godly child requires godly responses by both the parents and the child. When one or the other is lacking, failure often results.

But Manoah was still not aware of the identity of the visitor who had brought such startling news. In response to Manoah's question, "What is your name?" the angel did three things to reveal his identity.

● First, we note the response of the angel of the Lord is both mysterious and marvelous, "Why do you ask my name, seeing it is wonderful?" (v. 18) (The noun form of this adjective is rendered "wonderful" in Isaiah 9:6, a prophecy regarding the Messiah.)

● Second, to further reveal his identity the angel of the Lord "performed wonders" in the presence of Manoah and his wife (v. 19).

● Third, the angel then ascended to heaven in the flame that blazed up from the altar of sacrifice. As they watched this fearful event, Manoah and his wife came to realize they had seen God.

What an unusual day for this young couple! Not only did they learn they were to have a son born by God's miraculous intervention, but they also came to know his birth was announced by God's preincarnate Son, the Angel of Yahweh. There are profound spiritual lessons here for parents or parents-to-be.

It is touching to notice how Manoah's wife quickly shared her secret with her husband, and how they were both so deeply concerned about the child whom they were to have, and that the annunciation of Samson ended in worship by his parents to be. The coming of children into a home often brings parents into a new relationship with God. Men and women who have found little time for the church in their own lives seem to recognize the importance of spiritual training for their children.[6]

The birth and early development of Samson, 13:24-25. The promise of the angel was fulfilled, and a son was born to Manoah and his wife. They named him Samson meaning "little son," from the word, *shemesh,* meaning "sun." Approximately two miles away across the valley of Sorek was Beth-shemesh where the sun god was worshiped. Manoah, however, was not a worshiper of the sun god and may only have given his son a name common at the time. Someone has even suggested that the name means "sunny-boy" and that during his childhood days the lad no doubt brought joy and sunshine into the home of this previously childless couple. Sadly, during Samson's adult years he brought more sorrow than sunshine to his parents.

The child Samson grew up under the blessing of the Lord, as did another Nazirite, John the Baptist (see Luke 1:80). One day as Samson approached young manhood, the Spirit of the Lord came upon him and began to stir him, that is, impel and empower him for the work he was to do (v. 25). This seems to be the time when Samson first became physically strong, for there is no evidence he was born with this unique strength.

This narrative provides an illustration of the Holy Spirit's ministry to people in Old Testament times as contrasted with New Testament times. In the Old Testament period the Holy Spirit came upon individuals to empower them for special service; He did not permanently indwell them. In the New Testament period and throughout the church age, the Holy Spirit permanently indwells the life of the believer (John 14:16-17).

The Holy Spirit's ministry in the life of Samson was very significant as the following passages demonstrate: Judges 13:25; 14:6; 14:19; 15:14.

At this point in Samson's life, we would have to declare he was a highly favored man with tremendous promise for usefulness to God and His people. What more, in fact, could God have done for Samson?

• His birth was announced by an angel.

• He was born to godly and loving parents.

• He was dedicated to God at birth and set apart as a Nazirite for special service.

• As he grew, he experienced the special blessing of the Lord.

• The Holy Spirit endowed him with unique strength for his special mission against the Philistines.

But spiritual privilege is no guarantee of spiritual success. Paul applies this principle to the entire nation of Israel in the early verses of 1 Corinthians 10 as he recounts the numerous privileges of the Israelites and their repeated failures, closing with the somber warning: "Therefore let him who thinks he stands take heed lest he fall" (v. 12).

The marriage of Samson, 14:1-20. Chapter 14 introduces us to Samson as a man and stands as a depressing contrast to the events accompanying his birth and early life as recorded in the previous chapter. Four events are recorded here and combine to show us some flaws of character that kept Samson from being all God intended him to be.

• Samson meets the woman of Timnah (vv. 1-4). One day Samson walked about four miles westward down the valley of Sorek to the village of Timnah, and there he saw a beautiful, young Philistine woman. It was lust at first sight. In the Israelite society the father was recognized as the head of the family and as such chose wives for his sons. But Samson made his own choice and hurried home to break the news to his parents. Gary Inrig re-creates the scene:

"Well, Mom and Dad, I have seen the girl of my

dreams. She looks terrific. That is the girl I want to marry, so will you get her for me, make all the arrangements?"

"Oh, I am glad you have found the girl the Lord has for you, son. Who is she?"

"She is a Philistine girl from Timnah."

And with that statement Samson's parents' world fell apart. His parents knew all about his miraculous birth, God's call for his life, and for years they had been praying for him, that God would use their son to deliver Israel. Now their son, whom God had called to live a life of separation, wanted to marry one of the enemy. That was not only a betrayal of his calling, it was direct disobedience to the word of God, because God had told these people not to intermarry with the pagan people who lived in the land (Deut. 7:3-4). Immediately, Manoah tried to talk some sense into his son, "Is there not a single Hebrew girl you could marry? Do you really have to marry a Philistine girl? Those people are uncircumcised. They are outside of God's covenant. Does God's program not mean anything to you? Oh, Samson, you cannot marry her."

And Samson replied in a single sentence that tells an immense amount about the character of the man, "Get her for me, for she looks good to me."

As nothing else could, that simple sentence epitomizes the kind of man Samson was.[7]

Apparently, Samson had not even met the young Philistine girl. He chose a wife solely on the basis of what he had seen, solely on the basis of physical appearance, ignoring both the authority of God and the authority of his father. He "did that which was right in his own eyes." How ironic were Samson's words to his parents that he had seen a woman who looked good to him when those very eyes would be put out because of the betrayal of another eye-pleasing woman.

It is difficult to understand how this marriage could have

been "of the Lord" (v. 4). How could such a marriage, contrary to God's laws, be in any sense from the Lord? The sacred historian views the proposed marriage in the light of its results. That is, the outcome would bring the destruction of Israel's enemies. God disapproved of Samson's desire to marry this woman but purposed to overrule Samson's disobedience for His own glory. Similarly, God can and does overrule our foolish mistakes and our sins to accomplish His purposes. This fact, however, can never be used as an excuse or justification for doing wrong.

● Samson kills a lion (vv. 5-9). This event includes two trips Samson made to Timnah. Samson persisted in his demands to take the young girl as his wife, and his parents accompanied him to Timnah to make arrangements for the wedding. At a time when Samson was temporarily separated from his parents, he was suddenly accosted by a young lion. He felt a sudden surge of strength as the Spirit of the Lord came upon him, and he killed the lion with his bare hands. David and Benaiah would also kill lions, but only Samson was able to tear a lion apart as "one tears a kid." On festive occasions an Arab host would tear apart a kid of the goats before his guests, but superhuman strength was required to divide the body of a lion with bare hands. Perhaps Samson looked at his hands after the fierce encounter, scarcely able to comprehend the power God had given him.

After visiting his future wife, he returned home but later traveled back to Timnah for the wedding. On the way he stopped by the location where he had killed the lion and discovered that a swarm of bees had produced honey in the lion's carcass. Honey was a special delight to the ancients, and Samson not only ate some but took some for his parents. Samson did not mention the lion.

The story of Samson and the lion has been memorialized in literature and art. Author Maxine Hancock describes a painting entitled *Samson and the Lion* by Peter Paul Rubens:

[The painting] shows Samson in the beauty and power

of muscled youth, grappling a lion by the jaws, illustrating the instance told in Judges 14:5, 6. The lion's head is pulled back by Samson who bows over with the strain, so that man and lion create a circular configuration in the center of the canvas. More than just a picture of 'mighty opposites' in conflict, the presentation is symbolic, for Samson's conflict with passion was much like his struggle with the lion as pictured by Rubens. In the painting, the tension between the antagonists is unresolved. The structure is circular, so that it is easy to imagine the picture turned upside down to show the lion on top of Samson, as passion and desire dominated that man throughout his adult life.[8]

While this remarkable story may well mirror the struggle in Samson's life with the lust of the flesh, the story also shows that during his career Samson demonstrated great physical strength but great moral weakness.

● Samson prepared a wedding feast (vv. 10-18). Once again Samson returned to Timnah with his father to set in motion the wedding feast, a celebration of seven days after which the marriage was to be consummated. The Hebrew word for feast indicates this was a "drinking feast." (Hardly a suitable environment for a Nazirite who was committed to avoid all intoxicating beverages.) The presence of Samson's father is unexplained. Was he there in a last desperate attempt to stop a marriage he could not sanction? On the other hand, could it be that the father came out of sympathy because none of Samson's Israelite friends wanted to be involved in a marriage with one of their enemies? In the absence of Samson's own friends, the Philistines provided thirty of their number to function as groomsmen. This number indicates either an unusually large wedding or that they were appointed to provide protection against Samson.

In his exuberance Samson threw out a wager to the groomsmen, "Answer this riddle within the seven days of the feast," he said, "and I will furnish you thirty linen undergarments and thirty festive robes. If you cannot explain the riddle, you must furnish the same for me."

Samson's riddle was in the form of a couplet. Paired with the answer, it provides a beautiful example of Hebrew poetry and parallelism:

> Out of the eater came something to eat,
> And out of the strong came something sweet. (v. 14)
> What is sweeter than the honey?
> And what is stronger than a lion? (v. 18)

The groomsmen accepted the challenge, but as they pondered the riddle day after day, they concluded that it was unanswerable and that Samson indeed was mocking them. As the seventh day arrived, the atmosphere was tense and bitter, and the groomsmen approached Samson's wife with an ugly threat, "Get us the answer to Samson's riddle or we'll burn your house down with you in it."

Samson's bride was in a terrible predicament, and she determined her only way out was to persuade Samson to reveal to her the meaning of the riddle. In keeping with what someone has stated as a standard rule for brides: when in doubt, cry, she wept in the presence of Samson. Through her tears she strongly implied that if Samson truly loved her, he would keep no secrets from her. The bridal tears melted Samson's heart, and he capitulated, telling his bride the answer to the riddle. She in turn quickly passed the answer on to the groomsmen, who flung the answer in Samson's face just as the feast was coming to an end and the marriage was about to be consummated. Using a coarse metaphor Samson replied,

> If you had not plowed with my heifer,
> You would have not found out my riddle (v. 18).

These sharp words contained a double rebuke—a scornful reference to his wife and a charge that the groomsmen had used a devious device to secure the answer to his riddle.

● Samson slaughters thirty Philistines (vv. 19-20). In a rage Samson left the wedding and stormed to Ashkelon on the Mediterranean coast. There he felt the supernatural power of the Spirit of the Lord come upon him, and he killed thirty Philistines, stripped them, and took the tunics and robes he needed back to Timnah where he hurled them at the feet of his treacherous groomsmen. Then, because his intense anger had dissipated any desire for his bride, he petulantly stalked to his parents' home. Meanwhile, because it was considered a disgrace for a bride to be deserted in this fashion at the completion of the wedding festivities, she was given to Samson's best man who consummated the marriage.

Conclusion
Reviewing Judges 13 and 14, we see we have been introduced to one of the most unusual characters of the Bible. Born by God's direct intervention, Samson was nurtured by godly parents, blessed by God as he grew to manhood, divinely appointed to an important ministry, and equipped by the Holy Spirit with the physical strength he needed to carry out his mission in life. Clearly, Samson lacked nothing. Yet, for all his resources and potential, Samson was a weak man. He failed to discipline himself and squandered all God had provided.

What a tragedy of our day that so many Christian leaders have not learned from Samson's failures. They have instead followed his sordid example to the ruination of their effectiveness as servants of Christ.

Every believer needs to be reminded that God has given us tremendous resources. Paul declared, "God . . . has blessed us with every spiritual blessing in the heavenly places in Christ" (Eph. 1:3), and Peter declared, "His divine power has granted to us everything pertaining to life and godliness" (2 Peter 1:3). It is up to us to realize and claim our riches in Christ. We must avoid the dangers of self-indulgence and halfhearted commitment to the lordship of Jesus Christ. Drawing on our immense God-given resources is the only way to live an abundant and victorious Christian life.

TEN

SAMSON: PASSION'S SLAVE

Judges 15–16

In the Shakespearian play *Hamlet*, the lead character says,

Give me that man
Who is not passion's slave (3.2).

Samson, Israel's enigmatic judge, does not qualify. His life was one of uncontrolled passion. Maxine Hancock writes:

He was a man described in Milton's *Samson Agonistes* as "designed for great exploits," but the record of his life is one of uncontrollable lust and savage fits of temper rather than exploits which would rank him with the great. His life is marked by paradox. He had great physical strength but this main inner weakness. "O, impotence of mind, in body strong," Milton has Samson bemoan himself. A man of considerable verbal cleverness—witness his riddles and proverbs—and ingenuity in gaining personal vengeance, he nonetheless ended life "deserving contempt . . . to be . . . avoided as a blab, the mark of fools set on his front." Another paradox is that of a man who under life-long Nazirite vows who, while observing at least some of the accompanying taboos, yet indulged in many kinds of carnality. The paradoxes culminate at the end of his life: the deliverer is delivered to his enemies, God's chosen scourge is beaten and blinded, the practical joker becomes a joke for revelling Philistines, and finally the dying Samson kills more Philistines than the living one ever had.[1]

The story of the man with unbridled passion and uncontrolled temper continues. The previous episode described how Samson's young Philistine bride responded to a Philistine threat to her life and betrayed her husband by revealing the secret of the riddle told at the wedding feast. Samson, in response, killed thirty men in Ashkelon, paid off his debt to the thirty Philistine groomsmen, and sullenly stalked home without consummating the marriage. Eventually, Samson's anger cooled and, not knowing his bride had been given in marriage to the best man at the wedding, he returned to Timnah to claim her.

Samson's Exploits at Timnah (15:1-8)

When Samson returned to Timnah, he brought his wife a goat as a present. The goat was probably not a gift of reconciliation—the equivalent of flowers, perfume, or candy in our modern age—but was no doubt the gift of the visiting husband in a *sadika* marriage. This form of marriage (still found among Palestinian Arabs) is characterized by the bride remaining with her parents and the husband coming to visit periodically as a guest. When Samson was faced with the shocking fact that his bride had been given to another groom, in a searing rage, he determined to attack the Philistines who had cruelly pressured the girl to turn her betrothal into a betrayal.

Boiling with anger, Samson walked down the valley of Sorek toward Philistine territory, gathering firebrands as he went. Catching a pair of jackals, he tied them tail to tail with the firebrand between. Lighting the firebrand, he released the terrified animals who ran to the Philistine grain fields for cover. Samson did not stop until he had captured, tied, and released 150 pairs of jackals, resulting in the grain fields, vineyards, and olive orchards becoming a virtual conflagration. (The Hebrew term for *foxes* may also be translated *jackals*. The latter are common in Palestine and are more easily caught than foxes since jackals run in packs.)

The Philistines were infuriated. An agricultural people, their livelihood and food supply for an entire year depended on the grain harvest. No doubt they also experienced some disillusionment since Dagon, the god of grain and the god of Philistia, was unable to prevent this catastrophe. The enraged Philistines went up to Timnah and burned alive Samson's wife and father-in-law because they had started the chain reaction ending in this disaster. What an ironic twist of fate—the very house Samson's bride attempted to save by betraying him was destroyed by fire, and she lost her own life in the process (see Jud. 14:15).

Samson was further enraged by this violent act of the Philistines and swore a further and final act of vengeance. (But the cycle did not end. It is hard to get off the treadmill of revenge and retaliation.) Samson tore into the mob of the Philistines and struck them down "leg on thigh" (literally, a Hebrew idiom for a complete or total massacre). Then, fearing further reprisals, Samson fled for refuge to a "cleft of the rock of Etam," believed to be a cave in the cliffs near Samson's home.

It is obvious Samson's temper was completely out of control. While these vicious acts weakened the Philistines, Samson's motives appear to be personal, satisfying his own sensual desires and avenging his injuries. James wrote, "The anger of man does not achieve the righteousness of God" (James 1:20). Samson's unbridled anger is but another illustration of his lack of self-discipline.

Samson's Exploits at Lehi (15:9-20)
Smarting under the slaughter of their countrymen at Timnah, the Philistines approached Lehi in the vicinity of Zorah to discover and conquer this one-man army once and for all. The

fact that the Philistine force included at least 1,000 men (15:16) acknowledges Samson's great strength and his continuing threat to the Philistines. The people of Judah were greatly alarmed over the coming of this strong enemy force and asked fearfully, "Why have you come up against us?" (v. 10) The Philistines relieved the fears of the men of Judah by reassuring them they had come only to capture Samson. Sadly, instead of resisting the Philistines and protecting Samson, the Israelites sent a 3,000-man force of their own to bring Samson back to almost certain death. Their actions clearly demonstrate that the Israelites had accepted the domination of the Philistines and lived in constant fear of being overrun and destroyed by this dreaded enemy.

Gary Inrig sees a vivid picture of the consequences of compromise in the Israelites' actions. He observes that the people had become thoroughly accommodated to the spiritual status quo. When the 3,000 men of Judah went to Samson's hiding place, they sharply rebuked him, "Do you not know that the Philistines are rulers over us? What then is this that you have done to us?" (v. 11) Clearly, the Israelites did not want to fight against the Philistines. They preferred a policy of peaceful coexistence and were greatly agitated by Samson's disturbing of the peace.

Is it possible twentieth-century Christians have sunk to the level where we too prefer slavery to freedom? It is all too possible for us to accommodate ourselves to the world's lifestyle and to make subtle compromises rather than to be firm in our commitment to God.

Dr. Francis Schaeffer notes that in our modern age the majority of people have adopted two values: personal peace and affluence.

> Personal peace means just to be let alone, not to be troubled by the troubles of other people, whether across the world or across the city—to live one's life with minimal possibilities of being personally disturbed. Personal peace means wanting to have my personal life

pattern undisturbed in my lifetime, regardless of what the result will be in the lifetimes of my children and grandchildren. Affluence means an overwhelming and ever-increasing prosperity—a life made up of things, things, and more things—a success judged by an ever-higher level of material abundance.[2]

Inrig notes that the Israelites were ignored by the enemy (v. 10). Since the people represented no threat, the Philistines made it clear they had no quarrel with them. As Christians today, we should be concerned if Satan ignores us. If Satan leaves us alone, we are not threatening his cause, and we are being less than effective in the Christian conflict with evil.

Finally, Inrig concludes that the Israelites were doing the enemies' work for them (v. 12). By capturing Samson, the men of Judah were indeed fighting the Philistines' battle. How tragic that the apathetic Christian who sits on the sidelines can actually aid the enemy and become a positive hindrance to the cause of Christ.[3]

Samson's response to the men of Judah was remarkable. In fact, on this day Samson not only experienced his greatest moment of triumph apart from the day of his death, but he also reached greater spiritual heights than at any other time in his life.

• Samson demonstrated concern for his fellow Israelites in connection with his agreement to surrender to them and be bound and led to the Philistines. He requested assurance they would not kill him themselves. Fully conscious of his God-given strength, Samson's request was not made out of fear but with the knowledge that if the men of Judah turned to harm him themselves, many of them would have suffered death. While Samson could have retaliated against the Israelites, he demonstrated he had their interest at heart. Here at least we see Samson controlling his volatile spirit.

• Surrounded by 3,000 Israelites, Samson courageously walked into the camp of the bloodthirsty Philistines, his ears ringing with their shouts of triumph. Who can question that only Samson's faith in God could produce such calm courage? For this, Samson was listed with the other heroes of faith in Hebrews 11.

● In response to Samson's faith, God gave him great victory over the enemy. Samson himself acknowledged this when he prayed, "Thou hast given this great deliverance by the hand of thy servant" (v. 18). Like electricity flowing through a conduit, Samson experienced the power of God's Spirit, snapped the new (and stronger) ropes, and picked up a fresh (and more supple) jawbone of a donkey from the ground to use as a terrible weapon. Singlehandedly he killed 1,000 Philistine soldiers. Leon Wood believes that the Philistines broke into a run when they saw him break the new ropes so easily:

> They wanted no part of anyone who could do such feats. But fleeing they became only easier prey for the mighty Samson, who no doubt was empowered to run rapidly in pursuit as well as fight fiercely. Small groups may have tried to stand as he caught up with them, thus making for the collections of the bodies in "heaps" as Samson described them. Finally, 1,000 lay dead as a result of Samson's enormous effort.[4]

Sadly, as the bloody conflict continued, there is no mention of any help from the apathetic men of Judah, who must have been eyewitnesses to the event.

● In the hour of his triumph, Samson uttered a prayer to God, the only one recorded prior to the prayer at the time of his death. This was a spiritual high point in the life of Samson as he cried out to God after the victory. In his prayer he acknowledged the victory was achieved by God working through him (v. 18). According to the angel, Samson would "begin to deliver Israel," and by this tremendous victory God enabled him for the task. In the prayer Samson acknowledged he was but the servant of the Lord, carrying out the mission God had given him in life. On this occasion, at least, Samson lived up to God's calling.

But the prayer was also a cry of despair. After such great exertion of energy, Samson—exhausted and thirsty—cried out to God, "You have used me to bring a great deliverance to Israel today, and are You now going to allow me to die of thirst?" A typically human scene! After a victory, we often fall victim to depression. It happened to the Prophet Elijah (1 Kings 19) after the triumph over the prophets of Baal on Mount Carmel, the seventeen-mile run from Carmel to Jezreel, and the journey of more than 120 miles to the country south of Beersheba. Exhausted and dejected, he slumped under a juniper bush and asked the Lord to take his life. How encouraging to observe God's recognition of our physical as well as our spiritual needs and His tender dealing with His depressed servants. God, in answer to Samson's prayer, split open a hollow place and water miraculously gushed out to assuage the consuming thirst and revive the sagging spirit of Samson.

Dr. Lewis Sperry Chafer, founder of Dallas Seminary, comments:

> We should not mistake worn nerves, physical weakness, or depression for unspirituality. Many times sleep is more needed than prayer and physical recreation than heart searching.[5]

The episode describing Samson's God-given victory over the Philistines closes with the notice, "So he judged Israel twenty years in the days of the Philistines" (v. 20). The same notice appears at the end of chapter 16. It would appear then that Samson functioned as a peacetime judge from the time of the killing of the 1,000 Philistines until the sinful episodes that led to the end of his life. We can infer that after the massacre, the Philistines suspended their attempts to capture Samson, and Samson himself ceased his raids against the Philistines. The events up to Judges 15:20 occurred in approximately one year; the events which began with Samson's relation with Delilah probably transpired in less than a year. This would mean that between Samson's early and later Philistine contacts he had approximately eighteen years of peacetime judging.

The scriptural record of Samson's undisciplined indulgence of the flesh is limited to the beginning and end of his career, but we cannot necessarily conclude these were his only sinful involvements. We must assume the writer of the Book of Judges was guided by the Holy Spirit to select those episodes most truly reflecting the character of this enigmatic but significant leader of Israel. At any rate, it is encouraging and instructive to note that when Samson reached the spiritual pinnacle of his life and walked in God's ways, God rewarded him with a great victory and gave Israel nearly twenty years of stability and peace. So today God rewards those who trust Him and obey His Word.

Samson's Exploit at Gaza (16:1-3)

Samson's exploits continued. After noting his physical and spiritual achievements in the previous section, how disappointing it is to see how he failed once again. Samson had a weakness for women, and he failed to overcome temptation in that area on more than one occasion. Ambrose, an early church father, commented:

> Samson, when brave, strangled a lion; but he could not strangle his own love. He burst the fetters of his foes; but not the chords of his own lust. He burned the crops of others, and lost the fruit of his own virtue when burning with the flame enkindled by a single woman.[6]

Probably near the end of Samson's time as judge he journeyed thirty-eight miles down the Sorek Valley from his home at Zorah to Gaza, one of the five leading cities of the Philistines, just three miles inland from the Mediterranean Sea. Why did he go? The reason is not stated, but perhaps he felt the Philistines once again needed to be reminded of his presence. Whatever may have motivated the visit, Samson soon fell into the clutches of a prostitute. Was she a "plant" by the Philistine leaders, or did the prostitute herself go out of her way to entice him? Whatever the reason, the temptation came at a time when Samson's spiritual life was at a low ebb. Apparently he saw no contradiction in being a servant of the Lord and also visiting a prostitute. Samson is sowing seeds in Gaza he will reap in Sorek with Delilah. He is on a pathway leading to his destruction. God would deal with him as He warned He would deal with Israel, reinforcing the principle that obedience will bring blessing and disobedience chastisement (Deut. 28).

When the Philistines discovered Samson was in the city, they made careful plans to trap and kill him. They posted guards both at the prostitute's house and at the city gate. They would wait for their prey and capture him in the morning light. This, of course, was contrary to all sound thinking if they had but recalled the Philistine massacre at Lehi. Perhaps enough years had passed to dim the Philistines' memory.

Eventually, the guards apparently relaxed their vigilance and were then, no doubt, paralyzed with fright when Samson appeared at midnight at the locked city gate. There he used his God-given strength to rip the gateposts out of the ground and carry off the entire gate structure (including the posts and bars).

Professor William Barrick has explored in depth the nature of this unusual feat of strength. Based on evidence from archeological digs at Hazor and Ashdod, he has determined the probable height and thickness of the gates and proposes that the gate had an approximate thickness of 3.3 feet, an approximate height of 9.9 feet, and a weight of approximately 10,696 pounds. A gate of minimum thickness (1.65 feet) would have weighed 5,350 pounds. Barrick states:

> These figures do not include the bar nor the bronze plating! If the plating were included, it would practically double the weight of the gates. . . . The gates of Gaza could well have weighed in the vicinity of five to ten tons! The deed definitely takes on miraculous proportions. The praise must go to Samson's God who supernaturally empowered him. . . . Samson did not lift the gates and put them down. He then proceeded to carry them from Gaza to the vicinity of Hebron (ap-

proximately thirty-six miles "as the crow flies"). The change in altitude involved approximately 3,200 feet (Gaza is about 100 feet above sea level and Hebron is about 3,300 feet above sea level). . . . In conclusion, the removal of the gates by Samson was indeed a miracle of unparalleled proportions. The computation of the gate's dimension and weight can only heighten the awe which the reader of Judges 16:1-3 possesses in the presence of this supernatural feat of strength. Only God's power could accomplish this deed through a mortal being. The God of Israel is truly mightier than the gods of the Philistines![7]

In ancient times a city was not considered secure without the gates in place (see Neh. 1–6). Gates were considered to be symbols of a city's strength. By removing the gates of Gaza then, Samson left the city in a state of humiliation and shame.

A difficult question remains. In view of the fact that Samson was committing a base sin by going into the prostitute, why didn't God remove his strength in punishment? The answer seems to be that God is a God of patience and long-suffering with His servants, and sometimes He will continue to use them for a time in spite of serious sin in their lives. Samson, however, had taken a tragic step downward and would soon reap what he had sown.

Samson and Delilah (16:4-22)

For the third time Samson became infatuated with a woman of Philistia. Only in this case do we read that Samson "loved a woman." She lived in the Valley of Sorek, and her name was Delilah, possibly meaning "flirtatious." Her name is recognized as a synonym for a seductive woman.

After the Gaza episode, the Philistines were reminded that Samson was still their nemesis, and yet they did not have the courage to attempt his capture until they learned the secret of his strength. Their determination to take Samson at this time is indicated by the fact that the five lords of the Philistines, rulers of the pentapolis, were taking the initiative. These lords offered Delilah a total of 5,500 pieces of silver for telling them the secret of Samson's strength, showing the depth of their desire for revenge. Of course, from Delilah's standpoint the risk was large and the bribe had to be significant enough to outweigh the danger to herself. Like Judas Iscariot, however, Delilah was willing to betray a friend for money. Samson, on the other hand, amazes us for his credulity and stupidity in not sensing his danger. No doubt he was blinded by his passion for Delilah. Gary Inrig comments:

> Samson thought playing with Delilah was a game. It turned out to be Russian roulette, and he bought the bullet. You cannot trifle with sin in your life. If you are like Samson, flirting with a Delilah, believing that you can keep sin inbounds, let me warn you that you are playing with a lion. You may stick your head in its mouth once and get away with it, even twice and three times. Samson did. But, one of these times, that lion will shut its mouth, and you will lose your head, once for all.[8]

● Going about her evil task in a cold and calculated manner, Delilah plied Samson for the secret of his strength. Samson replied that he should be tied with seven fresh bowstrings (RSV) made of twisted gut, and he would be as weak as any man. Delilah did as Samson had suggested and then said, "The Philistines are upon you, Samson!" With a burst of strength, Samson freed himself. While it has been suggested that on each of these occasions Samson killed the previously hidden Philistines when they burst in, it seems more likely the Philistines remained hidden until they could be sure his strength was gone.
● Discovering Samson had deliberately misled her, Delilah was upset and again asked Samson how he could be bound so he would be unable to escape. Samson suggested he be bound with new ropes, and then he would be weak as any man. The new ropes were provided, Samson was bound, and Delilah said,

"The Philistines are upon you, Samson!" As he had done when tied up with new ropes by the men of Judah (15:13), Samson snapped the ropes as though they were threads—and the Philistine men stayed hidden in the nearby room.

● The fateful game continued as Delilah again begged Samson to tell her his secret. With an arrogant and playful attitude Samson suggested Delilah weave seven locks of his hair into a piece of cloth already on the loom. As she began to weave the hair, Samson fell asleep. A third time Delilah shouted, "The Philistines are upon you, Samson!" Startled, Samson awoke and stood up, wrenching loose the entire loom. What a strange sight to see Samson walking about with the loom and the weaving hanging from his head!

● The unsuspecting Samson steadily moves headlong to his doom. John Hunter illustrates Samson's sheer stupidity with this story:

> Some time ago I was in a small country village in Scotland. I happened to pass by the place where animals were slaughtered for meat. I saw a small corral in which were a dozen hogs. I saw the man coming to kill these animals, and I wondered what on earth he would do. How could he capture them, for there were twelve, and they were all loose? But it was all so easy—he carried a bucket in which were some handfuls of tasty food and nuts such as hogs enjoy. First he threw a few of these nuts into the corral, and there were squeals of delight from the victims. Then he opened the gate and walked away, dropping a nut every so often. How those hogs enjoyed it! They scampered along behind him, heedless of where he was leading them. He used no whip or compelling force—they followed him of their own free will. I watched them disappear through an open door, which was closed behind them. They had danced their way to their death. So it was with Samson. Delilah simply "rattled the bucket" and he followed—to his death.[9]

● Thus far Delilah had been unable to worm the secret of Samson's strength from him. But she continued to nag him, even asking, "How can you say, 'I love you,' when your heart is not with me?" (v. 15) At last Samson capitulated and blurted out the secret of his strength, "A razor has never come on my head, for I have been a Nazirite to God from my mother's womb. If I am shaved, then my strength will leave me and I shall become weak and be like any other man" (v. 17). Delilah—now convinced Samson had told her the truth—sent for the lords of the Philistines, who apparently had given up and returned to their homes. They came, money in hand, to watch as a Philistine barber shaved off Samson's seven locks and left him bald. For the last time Delilah shouted, "The Philistines are upon you, Samson!" Samson jumped up to discover with chagrin that his strength was gone. Poor, lovesick, and deluded Samson laid that which was sacred in the lap of a treacherous woman.

But Samson lost more than just his hair; he lost the presence of the Lord. Some of the saddest words in all of the Bible are these: "But he did not know that the LORD had departed from him" (v. 20). Samson's strength was gone, and God was gone, not because Samson had been shaved (for the hair itself was not the source of Samson's unique strength). The uncut hair had demonstrated Samson's separation to the Lord from birth and his obedience to the Nazirite vow. Maxine Hancock comments:

> There is something inestimably sad about the departure of the Spirit of the Lord, as in the reluctant retreating of the Shekinah glory from the temple and the city, seen by Ezekiel (ch. 9-11). But there is something even more sad about a person so insensitive, so spiritually enslaved and blinded by his own desires, that he does not even know when the Spirit of the Lord has taken His reluctant and sorrowful leave. Samson, the strong man made weak by yielding to passion, did not even know that the Spirit of the Lord was gone.[10]

Quickly recognizing Samson's loss of his unique strength, the Philistines were able to carry out their long desire to capture their tormentor. First, they cruelly gouged out his eyes, and then they took him down to Gaza, the scene of one of Samson's earlier conquests. There, Samson was bound with bronze shackles and given the tedious task of grinding out grain in the prison. How far the mighty Samson had fallen! Not because God had failed him but because of his own failure due to uncontrolled pride and unbridled passion. God does not want us to miss the picture of Samson in 16:21.

But God did not abandon Samson. There is a glimmer of hope in the words, "However, the hair of his head began to grow again after it was shaved off" (v. 22).

The Scottish preacher Alexander Whyte believes Samson turned to God in the prison:

But man's extremity is God's opportunity. And in such words as were possible to Samson's Old Testament biographer, that sacred writer tells us that in Samson also where sin abounded, grace did much more abound, and that God's strength was made perfect in the day of Samson's weakness. That dark cell in Gaza—in Gaza, the scene of some of Samson's greatest sins—that shameful cell was a house of God, and a place of prayer and repentance to Manoah's overtaken and overwhelmed son. What a past Samson looked upon as he sat in the mill! What he might have been! What he might have done! How he might have departed to his fathers and left Israel! Three thousand years dissolve and *this* is Gaza. *This* is the mill with slaves. *This* man, and *that* man there, is Samson over again. Only, over again against light and truth that Samson never saw. "What profit is there in my blood," our Samson cries, "when I go down to the pit? Shall the dust praise Thee? Shall it declare Thy truth? Hear, oh LORD, and have mercy upon me. LORD, be Thou my helper. Turn my mourning into dancing, my dreaming into earnestness,

my falls into clearings of myself, my guilt into indignation, my sin into fear, my transgression into vehement
desire, and my pollution into revenge.[11]

And God heard the agonized and repentant cries of Samson.

The Death of Samson (16:23-31)

The imprisonment and removal of his eyes did not end the
humiliation of Samson. Some time after his capture the Philistines sponsored a service of national thanksgiving to Dagon,
their god, with the assembled lords and people proclaiming,
"Our god has given Samson, our enemy, into our hands"
(vv. 23-24). The people acknowledged the great harm Samson
had done to their country, describing him as "the destroyer of
our country, who has slain many of us" (v. 24).

Both the Israelites and the Philistines looked upon the struggle between them as a struggle between their deities. To the
Philistines, therefore, Israel's God had been defeated because
His champion had fallen. Samson's capture was Dagon's glory.
In remarks that are more pertinent today than they were when
they were originally written, the nineteenth-century English
expositor Alexander Maclaren asks:

> And is not all this true today? If ever some conspic-
> uous Christian champion falls into sin or inconsistency,
> how the sky is rent with shouts of malicious pleasure!
> What paragons of virtue worldly men become all at
> once! How swiftly the conclusion is drawn that all
> Christians are alike, and none of them any better than
> the non-Christian world! How much more harm the
> one flaw does than all the good which a life of service
> has done! The faults of Christians are the bulwarks of
> unbelief.[12]

It soon becomes apparent that the only reason the Philistines
had not killed Samson was because they wanted to make him
the object of laughter and scorn. As the excitement of the feast

reached its peak, the people (no doubt under the influence of the freely flowing wine) shouted for Samson to be brought forth to entertain them. Led by a small boy, Samson was brought out of the prison and forced to stand between the two pillars of the temple.

A letter written in January 1973 by James Monson, then Vice President of the American Institute of Holy Land Studies in Jerusalem, describes an archeological discovery that casts light on the construction of this temple:

> As you know, last summer our students dug at the ancient Philistine city of Tel Quasile under the direction of their archaeology instructor, Mr. Ami Mazar. As the excavation developed, a Philistine temple of the Biblical period was uncovered, built before or during the period of the Judges. This was the first temple of this type to be found here. What makes it so interesting is the unusual type of construction—*two large wood columns on stone bases only a few feet apart in the center of the temple*, next to the high place of the idol. They supported the rest of the mud-brick building. If you recall the story of Samson, the Philistines were celebrating his defeat and called him from prison to stand before their god. The Biblical writer tells us how Samson, by pushing on the two pillars, destroyed the building, the Philistines, and himself. For the fascinating details read Judges 16:23-30.[13]

In this kind of temple Samson entertained the howling Philistines—not by feats of strength but by degrading acts they forced him to perform. How sweet they considered their revenge. The mob numbered over 3,000 men and women, including the five lords of the Philistines. No doubt Delilah, their heroine, was also present. It appears that the officials and dignitaries were in a covered portion of the temple which looked out on the courtyard where Samson stood. The two pillars supported a roof that extended out into the courtyard. As the thousands of guests gloated over the blinded ex-hero's weakness and humiliation, Samson offered up a prayer to the true God, "O Lord God, please remember me and please strengthen me just this time, O God, that I may at once be avenged of the Philistines for my two eyes" (v. 28). Samson now realized his total dependence on God. He prayed. His prayer shows a man relying on the Lord and not on himself. He sought one final opportunity to serve God by destroying Philistines, and he asked God to empower him to do so.

Samson somehow knew the temple was so constructed that the fall of the pillars would bring the collapse of the building. He therefore grasped the two support pillars until they gave way and the building collapsed in ruin. While the exact number of casualties is not given, the text does state that more Philistines died at this time than all the Philistines Samson had slain during his lifetime—a number estimated in the vicinity of 1,100. Samson died too—not in an act of suicide but as a martyr who was willing to pay the price of death for victory over the enemies of God's people. Thus Samson's final act of vengeance helped fulfill his mission in life as announced by the angel to his mother, "He shall begin to deliver Israel out of the hand of the Philistines."

The Philistines' hatred of Samson would normally have led to abuse of his corpse (compare the treatment of King Saul's body in 1 Sam. 31:9-10). But the Philistines were probably in a state of confusion following the carnage caused by Samson and therefore allowed his brothers and family to remove the body from the temple ruins and bury it in the hill country overlooking the Valley of Sorek.

Lessons from Samson's Life

We cannot leave the gripping story of Israel's most enigmatic judge without pausing to consider what we can learn from his life. As it was said of Abel, "Samson being dead yet speaks." Ponder the following:

• The story of Samson warns us of the danger of toying with temptation. The Bible is clear in its exhortations: "flee immorality" (1 Cor. 6:18); "flee from idolatry" (1 Cor. 10:14); "but flee from these things, you man of God" (1 Tim. 6:11); "now flee from youthful lusts" (2 Tim. 2:22). Fleeing is never easy, but the alternative is to risk the danger of yielding to temptation.

Dietrich Bonhoeffer wrote a classic word on temptation:

> In our members there is a slumbering inclination towards desire which is both sudden and fierce. With irresistible power, desire seizes mastery over the flesh. All at once a secret, smoldering fire is kindled. The flesh burns and is in flames. It makes no difference whether it is sexual desire, or ambition, or vanity, or desire for revenge, or love of fame and power, or greed for money, or finally, that strange desire for the beauty of the world, of nature. Joy in God is . . . extinguished in us and we seek all our joy in the creature. At this moment God is quite unreal to us, He loses all reality, and only desire for the creature is real; the only reality is the devil. Satan does not here fill us with hatred of God, but with forgetfulness of God. And now his falsehood is added to this proof of strength. The lust thus aroused envelopes the mind and will of man in deepest darkness. The powers of clear discrimination and of decision are taken from us. The questions present themselves: "Is what the flesh desires really sin in this case?" "Is it really not permitted to me, yes—expected of me, now, here, in my particular situation, to appease desire?"[14]

● Samson's life confirms the truth of John 8:34, "Everyone who commits sin is a slave to sin." Paul echoes the same truth with the words, "Do you not know that when you present yourselves to someone as slaves for obedience, you are slaves of the one whom you obey, either of sin, resulting in death, or of obedience resulting in righteousness?" (Rom. 6:16) Samson, the man with such privileged beginnings, ended his life in servile toil, performing the humiliating duty of a beast of burden. The reason? Rather than resist evil, he surrendered and became its slave.

Edmund Burke spoke as follows of his beloved burden:

> Men are qualified for civil liberty in exact proportion to their disposition to put moral chains on their own appetites . . . society cannot exist unless a controlling power upon will and appetite be placed somewhere; and the less of it there is within, the more there must be without. It is ordained in the eternal constitution of things that men of intemperate minds cannot be free.[15]

● Samson is a picture of modern man whose slogans are, "Everyone is doing it so it must be right," and, "If it feels good, do it." The greatest rebellion of the present century is against the authority of God. Like Samson, modern man prefers to do what most pleases him.

Professor Allan Bloom has written a stinging indictment of the current generation of university students in his book, *The Closing of the American Mind.* Students today, he asserts, are not dedicated to learning or to serving their fellowman but to hedonism, promiscuity, and the refusal or inability to distinguish between forms of behavior. They have, says Bloom, been corrupted by moral relativism following the dictum of Nietzsche who said, "Without God, everything is permitted."

● Samson challenges us to use the gifts and talents we have for God's glory and not for selfish ends. Samson was given so much—yet he used it so selfishly. Dr. James Packer in a lecture on our seminary campus said,

> Samson is the Popeye of the Bible. He had a fantastic sense of humor, but he was short on character. He was a charismatic who concentrated only on his gifts.

As we contemplate the gifts God has given us, may we use them—not abuse them. Peter wrote, "As every man hath received the gift, even so minister the same one to another, as good stewards of the manifold grace of God" (1 Peter 4:10, KJV).

For all his faults and failures, Samson made a contribution to the welfare of his people, though it was not as great as it might have been because of compromise and carnality. May God keep us from yielding to carnal lusts that rob us of effectiveness in God's service.

ELEVEN
THE MARKS OF
MAN-MADE RELIGION
Judges 17–18

In his book, *The Closing of the American Mind*, Allan Bloom relates an incident that took place on the campus of his university. In a classroom session students were discussing the sexual revolution. The professor asked why parents no longer seem concerned about students living together without being married when once they protested vigorously if their children became involved in casual sex. A coed responded, "Because it's no big deal."[1]

Herbert London, New York University dean and author of *Armageddon in the Classroom*, concludes that the media is having a profound effect on today's young people. In a newspaper column he asks, "Do the ends justify the means? Yes, say writers for television programs and, yes, say students who watch television regularly. The bounds of behavior have been stretched to corporate deceit, adultery, blackmail—behavior frequently condoned on television. I had not realized how far down the slippery slope of moral relativism we have come."[2]

Honored theologian and author Dr. Carl F.H. Henry documents the evidences of American society crumbling:

Television networks that define good programming by

audience ratings, Wall Street's accommodation of
greedy inside traders, government-sponsored lotteries
that foist 'get-rich-quick' delusions on low income families, drug addicts numbering some 70 million, a crime
rate second only to that of Beirut, Lebanon, the world's
highest divorce rate, a multitude of co-habiting
unmarrieds, a million teenage pregnancies annually—
are we to shun these realities as patriotic unmention-
ables, or do we deplore them as disturbing evidence of a
nation moving perilously toward sunset, despite a contingent of 50 million evangelicals, all too many of
whom, like Lot's wife, may linger for a titillating
glimpse of Sodom?[3]

As twentieth-century America seems to have forgotten God,
so did ancient Israel in the period of the Judges.

For sixteen chapters in the Book of Judges, we have observed
the downward spiral of the Children of Israel in terms of rebellion, retribution, repentance, and restoration. The cycle
seems to repeat itself endlessly. In these sixteen chapters the
focus is on the deliverers whom God in compassion raised up to
deliver His people from the invaders: Othniel, Ehud, Deborah,
Gideon, Jephthah, and Samson. The emphasis in the last five
chapters of the Book of Judges differs in character from the rest
of the book. No foreign invasions are recorded in these chapters, and the repeated statement—the Israelites "did that which
was evil in the sight of the LORD" is replaced by the observa-
tion, "In those days there was no king in Israel; every man did
what was right in his own eyes" (17:6; 21:25; see also 18:1 and
19:1).

Two general stories describe the consequences of the people's
sinful departure from the worship of Yahweh and their accep-
tance of Canaanite Baal worship. Though these stories are included at the end of the book, they probably did not occur
chronologically at the end of the Judges period. A number of
Bible students have suggested the events took place in the days
of Othniel, the first judge, because of the presence of Jonathan,

grandson of Moses, in 18:30, the presence of Phinehas, son of Eleazer in 20:28, and the reference to the ark at Bethel (20:27-28). Together the two stories depict religious apostasy, moral collapse, and political anarchy.

The Idolatry of a Family (17:1-13)

Chapter 17 of the Book of Judges relates the sad story of what happened in the life of an individual and his family as a result of departing from God and abandoning His revealed truth. John J. Davis describes these results in terms of religious syncretism (the blending together of different religious ideas into one system), moral relativism, and extreme materialism.⁴ Specifically, Micah—leading character of the chapter—committed at least three sins: he stole from his mother; he established an idolatrous worship; he established a false priesthood.

Micah's theft from his mother, verses 1-2. We are first introduced to Micah whose name means, "Who is like Yahweh?" In spite of his name, Micah was a thief, having stolen 1,100 shekels from his mother. Apparently he was raised in a wealthy home where money was plentiful. The fact that the amount stolen was 1,100 shekels has led some to the conclusion that Micah's mother was Delilah (see Jud. 16:5), but evidence is lacking for such a view. We can assume, however, that thievery was probably a characteristic of everyday life in Israel since the Law of God had been largely abandoned and its principles forsaken. That Micah had indeed stolen a small fortune is indicated in verse 10 where the Levite was quite pleased to get a position which paid him ten pieces of silver a year!

Having heard his mother pronounce a curse on the thief, Micah was frightened into returning the money to her. In the ancient world people believed implicitly in the power of such curses, and the curse of a parent was considered especially powerful. Micah's mother responded to his confession by pronouncing a blessing, which was believed to countermand the curse. Perhaps the reason this mother did not harshly condemn her son was because she too was a thief, as the next section indicates.

Micah's idolatrous worship, verses 3-6. After receiving the silver, Micah's mother immediately weighed out 200 shekels—and 200 shekels only—and hired a silversmith to fashion an image and an idol. (One was probably carved out of silver, and the other one cast from molten silver.) Although she declared she had dedicated it all to the Lord, we must note that she kept back most of the silver, as did Ananias and Sapphira (see Acts 5:1-11). Micah then set up a shrine or a "house of gods" and added an ephod (see Jud. 8:27) and teraphim, probably effigies of Syrian deities. To complete this highly irregular religious scene, Micah appointed one of his own sons to serve as priest.

We can make a number of observations regarding Micah's actions.

First, he was grossly ignorant of what the Scriptures laid down regarding Israelite worship (see Ex. 20:4-16).

Second, we can see the clear influence of Canaanite practices on Micah. The Canaanites worshiped with the aid of images at local sanctuaries called high places.

Finally, Micah was living a life of religious syncretism, the blending together of Canaanite practices and the traditional worship of Yahweh. Micah was not worshiping Baal or any other false god. Rather, he intended to worship Israel's God with his idols. But God's condemnation of idolatry forbids not only the worship of false gods but also the worship of the one true God by images. John Calvin declared:

> A true image of God is not to be found in all the world and hence His glory is defiled, and His truth corrupted by the lie, whenever He is set before our eyes in visible form. Therefore to devise any image of God is itself impious; because by this corruption His majesty is adulterated and He is figured to be other than He is.[5]

The tragedy of Micah's actions is intensified when we remember that Shiloh (the site of the tabernacle) was also in the hill country of Ephraim, probably only a short journey from the house of Micah. The story illustrates a powerful inclination in the human heart toward idolatry. One of the final exhortations of Scripture came from John the Apostle, "Little children, guard yourselves from idols" (1 John 5:21).

The author of Judges adds a crucial word of explanation as to how such religious irregularities were allowed to take place: "In those days there was no king in Israel; every man did that which was right in his own eyes" (17:6). No doubt the author lived during a monarchy when such lawlessness was not permitted. He declares in effect, "That kind of king, so the argument goes, would have put a stop to such bastard worship."[6] The kind of king the author of Judges referred to was a theocratic ruler, faithful to the God of Israel and His revelation to the chosen nation. When Micah rejected God's Laws as the standard of conduct, only subjective norms remained: he determined right or wrong on the basis of his own evaluation. It was this moral and spiritual relativism which led to the dark ages of the Judges.

ABC-TV moderator Ted Koppel, in a commencement address at Duke University, said,

> We have actually convinced ourselves slogans will save us. Shoot up if you must, but use a clean needle. Enjoy sex whenever and with whomever you wish but wear a condom. No! The answer is no. Not because it isn't cool or smart or because you might end up in jail or dying in an AIDS ward, but because it's wrong. . . . In its purest form, truth is not a polite tap on the shoulder, it is a howling reproach. What Moses brought down from Mount Sinai were not the Ten Suggestions.[7]

So the lesson is clear. If people do what's right in their own eyes, they will end up doing what is wrong in the eyes of God. People will not just hit bottom morally, they will break clean through with gross idolatry, immorality, brutality, injustice, etc. This is inevitable when God's objective standards of truth and right and wrong are discarded.

Micah's priest, verses 7-13. A visitor came to Micah's shrine, a Levite from Bethlehem who is identified in 18:30 as the grandson of Moses. (Most Bible students agree the scriptural versions reading "the son of Manasseh" are incorrect and represent an attempt to disassociate Moses from this idolatrous Levite). The young Levite, Jonathan, was apparently unemployed and wandering through the land seeking a place of service and support. According to the Law of Moses, Levites were to be supported by the offerings of the people of Israel, so Jonathan's lack of support is further evidence of the apostasy that gripped the land.

When Micah met Jonathan the Levite, he immediately offered him a job, with salary, accommodations, and fringe benefits. Jonathan eagerly accepted the offer, evidence that the Levite too was determined to please himself rather than please God. He obviously knew the Law of Moses and its clear prohibitions with regard to idolatry. What a stark reminder—godly ancestors do not guarantee godly descendants. Every generation must make its own decision to follow the Lord and His Word.

Now that Micah had his idols, his shrine, and a Levite employed as his priest, he was sure God would prosper him. Micah was apparently sincere, but he did not conform to the truth. Like Micah, many today are sincere but misguided in their religious activity. They fail to measure everything against the teaching of God's Word, and as a result, they are led dangerously astray. As Carl F.H. Henry reminds us,

> American society is being penetrated as never before by alien religious influences that the West unhesitatingly once called pagan. Even witchcraft is practiced much as in pre-Christian society; demonism and satanic cults are likewise on the increase. Various forms of Oriental religions call harried and affluent Westerners to quiet meditation and self-denial. Refugees and immigrants from around the world have given new prominence to assorted religious practices. Mosques, shrines, and temples now dot our cities alongside the more traditional worship centers.[8]

The Idolatry of a Tribe (18:1-31)

It seems apparent there is a direct relationship between the story of Micah and the story of the migration of the tribe of Dan. The record of Micah's idolatry is graphically explained in order to show how the tribe of Dan became an idolatrous tribe.

The Danites search for living space, verses 1-10. The tribe of Dan was pressed for lack of space. Even though they had a military potential of 64,400 men (Num. 26:43), they were unable to occupy the territory allocated to them (Josh. 19:41-46; Jud. 1:34). Their failure to drive out the Ammorites was due not to lack of power but to lack of faith. The tribe therefore had two choices: to repent of their unbelief and claim the promise of God as they battled their enemies, or to look for a new territory where the occupants would be unprepared and vulnerable to attack. The tribe of Dan chose the easy way, but it was not the way of faith.

Soon after the five Danite spies began their journey northward to search out new territory, they came across the home of Micah where they encountered Jonathan, the young Levite. They recognized Jonathan—either because of some previous contact or because of his accent—and identified him as coming from the southern region of Judah. When the spies sought professional advice and God's blessing for their journey, the Levite granted it; however, a question must be raised about the source of the priest's assurance that God would prosper them. Living as he did in a paganized society, did he use some medium or sorcery? Continuing their journey of exploration, the spies came to the city of Laish where they found exactly what they were looking for. It was a lush area and the inhabitants were isolated from their neighbors and had formed no defensive alliances in case of attack. They could easily be conquered.

As a frequent visitor to Tell Dan and the beautiful Tell Dan nature reserve, I agree with the conclusions of Arthur Lewis:

> Travellers who have visited the Huleh Valley and the vicinity of Dan expound on the natural resources and fertility of the area. Water comes from every rock and

hill, pouring down from the nearby mountains of Lebanon. Like Scotland, this part of Galilee is green and
overgrown with all forms of vegetation. The tribe of
Dan had seized upon a veritable paradise on earth!⁹

Returning home jubilantly, they brought a unanimous and
enthusiastic report to their brethren, urging them to join the
migration northward.

The Danites despoil Micah's sanctuary, verses 11-26. In response to the report of the spies, 600 fighting men along with
women and children started for Laish. Since the Danites numbered 64,400 in the census just before the conquest of the land
(Num. 26:42-43), it is surprising this party of two or three
thousand people is so small. Scholars have suggested that the
tribe was decimated from its years of fighting the Amorites or
that the majority decided to remain where they were rather
than join the group of adventurers. In light of verse 19, however, it seems better to believe this was merely the first contingent, and once Laish was conquered the rest of the tribe would
follow.

After stopping at Kiriath-jearim in Judah the first night, the
fighting force and their families moved on to the vicinity of
Micah's house at Mount Ephraim. As they came to the shrine
of Micah, the 600 armed men stood outside while the five spies
greeted the Levite, then pushed their way past him, and began
to gather all of the booty they could find, especially the religious paraphernalia—the carved image, the molten image, the
ephod, and the teraphim. Their reasoning might have been, "It
would be a good idea to take some religion to our new location.
We will be far removed from the tabernacle at Shiloh, and this
is an opportunity to establish a substitute religion."

The response of the priest was weak and pointless, "What are
you doing?" The Danites in turn offered the priest an opportunity for promotion—from being the religious leader for a limited number of people to exercising the same function for an
entire tribe. Opportunist that he was and lacking any sense of
loyalty to Micah, the mercenary Levite gladly accepted the

offer. After all, his religious services were available to the highest bidder.

When Micah returned home, he was horrified to find his house of gods empty and his priest gone. Assembling his neighbors to help him, he pursued the Danites to retrieve his gods. When he had overtaken the Danites, Micah voiced his pathetic protest, "You have taken away my gods which I made, and the priest, and have gone away, and what do I have besides?" (v. 24) How sad that an Israelite should assume he could make a god. How strange that a man should have to rescue his god. How utterly deplorable that Micah's whole life was wrapped up in his house of gods and that he considered he had nothing left!

The men of Dan responded harshly, "Don't give us an argument, Bud, or we may just knock you down and kill you." Poor Micah realized his hopeless situation against a fighting force of 600 Danites, and so with a heavy heart, he returned to his empty house and empty life. Micah was a disillusioned and misguided Israelite who forsook the faith of his fathers and justly suffered the consequences of his grievous apostasy.

The Danites seize Laish, verses 27-31. Continuing on to Laish, the 600 Danites made short work of the peaceful and unsuspecting inhabitants—slaughtering the people and burning the city. It has been suggested that the attack on Laish follows the patterns of Joshua's conquest of Jericho and Hazor, consigning the inhabitants to destruction and burning the cities to the ground. Laish was then renamed after Dan, son of Jacob, and father of the tribe of Dan. The rebuilt city has been memorialized in the expression "from Dan to Beersheba" (Jud. 20:1). In the rebuilt city the Danites established a sanctuary for the idols. Jonathan and his sons served as priests for the tribe of Dan "until the day of the captivity of the land" (Jud. 18:30), probably a reference to the early days of David's reign when he captured Israel from Ish-Baal and destroyed the religious sanctuary at Dan.

In concluding the narrative, the biblical author notes that the Danites set up a false worship center while the true worship center existed in Shiloh. Here is a double tragedy. The false worship in Dan served as a forerunner of the calf worship established later by Jeroboam I at Dan, an act contributing to the subsequent demise of the Northern Kingdom (1 Kings 12:28-29). Furthermore, the existence of true and false worship centers brought a division to the people of Israel. Some worshiped an idol while the remainder worshiped Yahweh. John Hunter comments:

> What a shocking thing to consider. There, over the hill, was the tabernacle, the holy place of the Lord of hosts. Moses had been responsible for erecting it. The brazen altar was there, and all sins could be forgiven and cleansed. The holy of holies was there, the one true center of worship and adoration. God's priests were there, ready to meet with those who came in humble worship. Micah should have gone there and met with the Lord in all sincerity and truth. The Levites should have been there serving in a humble capacity as a servant in the Tabernacle. But there was no Lord in their lives, and they spent their days trying to invent an alternative to God.[10]

The Only True Religion
We are told the latest synthetic diamonds are almost indistinguishable from genuine stones. On occasion, even jewelers have been deceived. The refraction index of the imitation stones is 2.409, almost equaling the 2.417 refraction index of a natural diamond. The cost per carat of the synthetic diamond is about one-thirtieth the price of a fine stone.

Synthetic, man-made religions continue to multiply on every hand, with the tragic result that many are deceived and led astray. But true Christianity allows for no substitutes or imitations. It provides the only way to God, and its teachings constitute the only true standards for righteous living. The uniqueness of Christianity is illustrated by the story of the Chinese Confucius scholar who was converted to Christ and later told this story:

A man fell into a dark, dirty, slimy pit, and he tried to climb out of the pit, and he couldn't. Confucius came along. He saw the man in the pit and he said, "Poor fellow, if he'd listened to me, he never would have got there" and went on. Buddha came along. And he saw the man in the pit and he said, "Poor fellow, if he'll come up here, I'll help him" and he too went on. Then Jesus Christ came and He said, "Poor fellow!" and jumped into the pit and lifted him out."

Biblical Christianity is the only true religion, and it alone presents the One who meets man's deepest needs for eternal life in God's presence and for a satisfying, fulfilling life in this world.

TWELVE

THE FRUITAGE OF NATIONAL APOSTASY

Judges 19–21

Order is freedom! Disorder is bondage!

> Moral permissiveness in the name of personal freedom
> is delusion in the first magnitude. To live on the basis
> "I do as I please" is to court disaster. Imagine a football
> game without rules. It wouldn't last ten minutes . . . if
> anyone would even bother to get involved. Imagine a
> busy intersection downtown without traffic lights. It
> would take hours or more to untangle the tie-up . . .
> and the longer it took the worse it would get as tempers
> were inflamed—people try to take matters into their
> own hands. Rules make the game—and rules are as
> basic to life as they are to games. Life is governed by a
> moral order instituted by God. Man violates that order
> to his own peril. Morality is not arbitrary . . . it is part
> of the natural law of the universe and as basic to life as
> gravity.[1]

In the period of the Judges the people often did not want to
live by the rules. They wanted to do only what pleased them.

The Book of Judges concludes with one of the most unsavory stories in all of Scripture. It has, in fact, been called,

> the sewer of Scripture . . . the most disgusting and de-graded story in the Bible, unredeemed by an admirable character or a noble act. To read these chapters is to be repelled by them, and you cannot help feeling rather dirty. It is almost as bad as reading a newspaper today.[2]

The Crime at Gibeah of Benjamin (19:1-28)

The first of the two concluding stories in the Book of Judges illustrates the shame of idolatry in a family and tribe. This final story describes the violence and immorality that prevailed in the land. The tribes of Ephraim and Dan were the focus of the previous story, but the focus now turns to the Benjamites. A Levite once again plays the leading role and the village of Bethlehem is also involved again. Just as the shame of Micah's apostasy is explained by the lack of a theocratic king in Israel so this sordid tale begins with the now familiar words which explain, excuse, or even apologize for these events: "Now it came about in those days when there was no king in Israel" (19:1).

The desertion of the Levite's concubine, verses 1-15. In the day when Israel had no human king, a Levite of the hill country of Ephraim took a concubine from Bethlehem in Judah. In ancient Israel a concubine, though considered a wife, did not enjoy the status belonging to a full marriage partner. The practice, though common, was never divinely approved. In this case the concubine returned to her father's house in Bethlehem, leaving her husband because she was "angry with him" (v. 2, RSV). Had she been morally unfaithful as the KJV translation states, the Levite would no doubt have had her executed since the penalty for adultery was death (Lev. 20:10). After a separation of four months, the Levite journeyed to Bethlehem, hopeful of a reconciliation. The Levite was received cordially by his father-in-law, and after a three-day visit made preparations to return home with his concubine/wife. The persuasive father-in-law twice persuaded the Levite to postpone his departure, but on the evening of the fifth day, the Levite insisted on leaving Bethlehem to journey homeward. Arriving at the city of Jebus (later called Jerusalem) after a journey of two or three hours, the Levite's servant strongly suggested they spend the night in that location. The Levite was reluctant to do so because the city belonged to foreigners—the Jebusites (how ironic is the Levite's hesitation because it was not foreigners but Children of Israel who perpetrated the horrible outrage against the concubine). A pagan enclave existed in the land at this time because Benjamin had failed to carry out its mission of conquering the Jebusite city allotted to it by Joshua (Josh. 18:16). The Jebusites remained in possession of the city until David and his men captured it and made it Israel's capital.

The traveling party moved on about four more miles. As the sun was going down, they approached Gibeah in the territory of Benjamin. Gibeah, or the modern Tell el Ful, would later become the birthplace and capital of Saul's kingdom (1 Sam. 10:26; 11:4). Turning aside, the travelers entered Gibeah and sat down in an open place—probably just inside the gate—expecting hospitality from inhabitants of the city. For what was apparently an extended period, they waited in vain as the people of Gibeah ignored the unwritten code of hospitality, a sacred duty in the East. This absence of hospitality on the part of the Benjamites was another outward sign of the apostasy of the day and was also an ominous warning of events to come.

The hospitality of an Ephraimite in Gibeah, verses 16-21. It appears the Levite and his party would have waited in vain near the city gate had not an old man, also a native of Ephraim, stopped to talk with them. The Levite assured the old man he had adequate supplies for his donkeys and the party of three, but the man brushed aside this suggestion, granting full hospitality to the weary travelers. He provided fodder for the donkeys, water for the travelers to wash their feet, and food to satisfy their hunger. With their fears relieved and their basic needs met, the Levite, his servant, and his concubine relaxed, only to have the gracious display of hospitality rudely interrupted.

The depravity of the men of Gibeah, verses 17-28. The interruption of the festivities came by the demands of a group of wicked men called literally "sons of Belial" (v. 22, KJV). This phrase of reproach is frequently used in the Old Testament and means literally "sons of no profit" or "sons of worthlessness." Specifically, it refers to those involved in idolatry, rebellion, and drunkenness. Here the phrase refers to lewd and sensuous men who pounded vigorously on the door and demanded, "Bring out the man who came to your house so we can have sex with him" (v. 22, NIV). The same demand was made of Lot when he entertained the angels in Sodom (Gen. 19:5). In fact, the point by point comparison to the angels and men of Sodom is no doubt designed to show how the moral cancer of the Canaanites had deeply penetrated the Hebrew society.

It is clear from Genesis 19 and Judges 19 that the contemporary homosexual movement is not new. Sadly, many cultures have embraced this form of sexual perversion. Gary Inrig states:

> Our society is filled with gross immorality, defended by suave, articulate, attractive spokespersons. You can scarcely find a perversion that someone is not willing to defend as essential to human freedom.[3]

The author of a publication advocating homosexuality expresses opposition to morals based on "the primitive revelations of the Bible" and calls for relief for "brothers and sisters who are victims of organized religion."[4]

In order to protect his guest from harm, the old man offered his virgin daughter and the Levite's concubine to the evil men of the city. To save his own skin, the Levite joined in the offer and allowed his concubine to be ravished and raped by the men of Gibeah. This grisly incident raises many questions. Why did the Levite and the old man put the conventions of hospitality above the care and protection of the weak and helpless? Why did the Levite show such a callous disregard for the one he professed to love by throwing her out to the mob? Why was homosexual rape considered unthinkable while heterosexual rape was thought to be acceptable? The bottom line is that individuals were ignoring the Law of God, doing what was right in their own eyes (and wrong in God's eyes). Thus a whole nation was led into moral collapse.

After a night of utter horror, the concubine collapsed and died on the threshold of her master's house. The Levite who had thrown the concubine out to a rabid mob to save himself now arises after a good night's sleep and prepares for the journey homeward. His harsh and curt words to the concubine, "Up and let us be going," show the Levite's absurd callousness and obliviousness to human suffering. At first unable to express any sense of outrage, he places the concubine's body on one of his donkeys and journeys home.

Though some might want to think this ugly story could only be acted out in a primitive society, modern illustrations of similar events belie that suggestion. While vacationing on the Gulf Coast, I found the papers filled with reports of the gang rape of a 19-year-old mother of two children by as many as twenty men. According to an authority on gang rapes, it was the largest such incident known to have occurred in the United States. Of particular concern was the fact that community leaders in attendance at a nearby illegal cockfight were aware of the sexual assault and did nothing to attempt to halt the assailants. There can be no denying that "the heart is more deceitful than all else and is desperately sick" (Jer. 17:9).

The War Against the Tribe of Benjamin (19:29–20:48)
The gross and perverted actions of the men of Gibeah led to Israel's first civil war, the consequence of which came perilously close to eliminating an entire tribe from the roster of God's people.

The summons of the nation, 19:29-30. Arriving home, the Levite cut the concubine's body into twelve pieces. The author employs a Hebrew word used to describe the process of dividing sacrificial offerings according to their bones. The twelve pieces symbolized the idea that the nation was divided into twelve somewhat independent and self-seeking tribes. He then sent the mutilated body from location to location throughout the tribes as an indictment of the spirit that produced such a crime and also as a warning that if the tribes did not avenge this wrong, they too might be hewn in pieces as was the murdered woman. It was a summons intended to arouse the nation to action and to render judgment on the guilty tribe. A similar summons to war was issued when Saul rallied the nation to support the men of Jabesh-gilead by dismembering a yoke of oxen (1 Sam. 11:1-8).

The Levite's desperate and grisly action had its desired effect. All who witnessed the gruesome corpse were shocked and declared this foul deed the greatest atrocity since the Exodus from Egypt. The latter part of verse 30 may be understood as the words spoken by messengers who took the pieces (or the entire mutilated body) to the twelve tribes and told the story of the depraved actions of the Benjamites in Gibeah. Some ancient Septuagint manuscripts state:

> And he commanded the men whom he sent out saying, "Say these words to all the men of Israel, has such a thing as this ever happened from the day when the children came up out of the land of Egypt until this day? Consider it, take counsel, and speak."[5]

The report to the tribes at Mizpah, 20-1:11. The Levite's call for an inquest brought results. All Israel, from Dan in the north to Beersheba in the south including representatives of the Trans-Jordanian tribes (Gilgal), assembled at Mizpah, a location only a few miles north of Gibeah. Only the men of Jabesh-gilead were missing (Jud. 21:8). The unity of the tribes at this stage in their history is noteworthy. The nation was outraged that such gross evil could be perpetrated by some of their own number.

It has been said that when a nation loses its sense of moral indignation for evil it is soon to fall. In this early phase of the Judges period, then, we see a glimmer of hope for Israel because the men of Israel knew the Law of God had been broken and judgment must be rendered.

When the Israelites assembled, the tragic and bizarre happenings at Gibeah were uppermost in their minds. "Tell us," they pleaded, "how did this wickedness take place?" Sadly, the Levite's speech was a self-serving one that presented his case in the best possible light. His speech stressed the personal pronouns *I* and *me*; in fact, only three times did he mention the murdered woman. The Levite actually distorted the facts by failing to mention he pushed his concubine out into the hands of the mob to save himself. He does not mention this is the reason "they ravished my concubine so that she died." Israel's verdict was unanimous. They would launch an attack against the city of Gibeah to punish the guilty parties. Lots were then cast to determine who should care for the food supplies for the armies.

The ultimatum to the Benjamites, 20:12-17. A plan of action was adopted and implemented immediately. Representatives of the tribes were sent throughout the territory of Benjamin to admonish the people for the atrocity and exhort them to produce the guilty men for punishment. According to the Law of Moses (Deut. 22:22), the rape of the Levite's concubine was a capital crime. God's Law commanded the death penalty for the guilty men of Gibeah, and only the implementation of God's Law would purge evil from the land.

The response of the Benjamites was deplorable. Rather than surrender a few guilty persons to justice, they stubbornly decided on an armed defense of the murderers, thus bringing judgment on the entire tribe. It is bad enough to commit a grievous sin but worse to defend it. Like many today, however, the Benjamites were unable to accept reproof. They would learn the hard way. "A man who hardens his neck after much reproof will suddenly be broken beyond remedy" (Prov. 29:1).

The odds in the forthcoming battle would seem to be clearly on the side of the armies of Israel numbering 400,000 men. The Benjamites mustered only 26,000 men armed with the sword and 700 men who were skilled marksmen with slings. The slings, however, were formidable weapons. As Arthur Cundall relates,

The *sling* which was employed with a left-handed motion must not be confused with the modern school boy's catapult; it was a formidable weapon of war used in the Assyrian, Egyptian, and Babylonian armies as well as in Israel. David's encounter with the Philistine, Goliath, is a telling example of the power and accuracy of this weapon (1 Sam. 17:49). It has been estimated that stones weighing up to one pound could be projected with uncanny accuracy at speeds up to 90 mph![6]

The conflict with Benjamin, 20:18-48. It was a grave moment. The tension was probably only paralleled by the tribal conflict after the conquest of the land as recorded in Joshua 22. Once again the horrors of a civil war hung in the balance.

In 1858 Abraham Lincoln and Stephen A. Douglas were engaged in debates in Illinois. On one occasion Lincoln took as his subject that a house divided against itself cannot stand. He argued that this country could not survive with slavery in the south and freedom in the north. After Lincoln's strong presentation, Mr. Douglas debated that the government could stand . . . half slave, half free. In rebuttal Mr. Lincoln is reported to have said,

> Mr. Douglas has taken this debate out of my hands. It is no longer between Mr. Douglas and me, it is now a debate between Mr. Douglas and the Man who spake as never man ever spake. Jesus Christ said, "A kingdom divided against itself cannot stand." If Stephen Douglas says it can stand, the debate is between him and the Man who spake as never man spake.[7]

● The first battle (vv. 19-23) between the Israelites and the Benjamites was fought only after men of Israel went to Bethel in search of God's will. Apparently, though the tabernacle was still at Shiloh, the ark was brought down to Bethel, only five miles north of Mizpah. Judah was designated to go into battle first, not only because of its size and fighting capability, but also because its hilly terrain was similar to that in the vicinity of Gibeah. The encounter at Gibeah resulted in the slaying of 22,000 Israelites. With heavy hearts the Israelites once again went up to the ark of the Lord in search of His will. Once again the Lord sent them into battle, and they prepared for their second encounter with Gibeah.

• The second battle (vv. 24-28) saw further losses inflicted on the Israelites as 18,000 fell in the conflict. Heartbroken, the Israelites returned to Bethel where they spent an entire day weeping, fasting, and offering burnt offerings (signifying complete surrender to God) and peace offerings (signifying they sought communion with God). While Israel's two defeats in battle are not explicitly explained, the defeats indicate that though Benjamin had sinned greatly, the other tribes were not without sin, and God's judgment had fallen on them. Some have suggested that Israel's failure to suppress the idolatry of the Danites is the major factor in turning the hand of God against them.

In response to the repentance of the Israelites, the Lord spoke through His priest, Phinehas, and promised victory in battle the next day.

• The third battle (vv. 29-48) brought a change in strategy on the part of the Israelites. Instead of a direct frontal assault as in the first two battles, Israel's strategy this time was to lure the Benjamites out into the open, destroy Gibeah by a force left in ambush, and then trap their enemy in a pincers movement. Joshua employed a similar ruse with outstanding success at Ai (Josh. 8:3-28).

This third phase of the warfare is described in a general account in verses 29-36a, followed by a more detailed description in verses 36b-46. The setting of the ambush around Gibeah is described first. The Israelites took up the same battle positions and then deliberately fled as the Benjamites attacked. Thus the Benjamites were drawn from Gibeah and met by 10,000 Israelite soldiers. In a bloody conflict the Benjamites lost 25,100 soldiers as God gave Israel the victory.

Details of the ambush and aftermath of this major battle then follow. After the Benjamites were drawn away from Gibeah, the Israelites in ambush easily took the city, killed the population, and set Gibeah on fire. The smoke of the burning city was a prearranged signal for the retreating Israelites to attack the Benjamites who then fled eastward to the desert. Only 600 Benjamites escaped to the rock of Rimmon, an area of ravines and caves where the surviving Benjamites could hide.

Judgment then fell on the remaining cities of Benjamin, since the entire tribe had failed to deliver the wicked men to the Israelites for judgment. In the carnage, human beings and cattle were destroyed. Since the Benjamites had copied the Canaanites in their sins, they received the same punishment.

The awful judgment on this city of Gibeah and the entire tribe of Benjamin is a foreboding commentary on the ultimate wages of sin. Lord Byron, a brilliant poet, spent his life in a mad search for pleasure. Toward the end of his days he wrote,

> The thorns which I have reap'd are of the tree I
>   planted;
> they have torn me, and I bleed.
> I should have known what fruit would spring from such
>   a seed.
> (*Childe Harold's Pilgrimage*, Canto W, Stanza 10).

Repopulation of the Tribe of Benjamin (21:1-25)

The remorse of the Israelites, verses 1-7. Though Gibeah had been punished for the gross sin committed in her midst, and the bloodguiltiness had been removed from the land of Israel by the deaths of over 25,000 Benjamites, the Israelites awakened to the sad realization that the tribe of Benjamin—with only 600 surviving men—was now threatened with extinction. Complicating the problem, at Mizpah the Israelites had made a rash vow not to allow their daughters to marry any Benjamites who might survive the impending conflict. The Law of Moses forbade the surviving Benjamites to marry Gentiles (see Ex. 34:16; Deut. 7:3). Where could Hebrew wives be found for the Benjamites so their tribe would not be completely exterminated?

The provision of wives for the surviving Benjamites, verses 8-24.
As the Israelites lamented before the Lord at Bethel, they
called to mind another solemn oath to impose the death penalty on any Israelites who had not responded to the summons to
Mizpah. When the leaders discovered that the people of Jabesh-
gilead, on the far side of Jordan, had not responded and therefore had not participated in the battle, they developed a
scheme to "kill two birds with one stone." They decided to
send an Israelite force to destroy Jabesh-gilead, thus fulfilling
the oath, and at the same time sparing a company of virgins,
who would subsequently be turned over to the surviving Benjamites. The victorious Israelite force returned to Shiloh with
their 400 young girls, terrified prisoners who were now or-
phaned and homeless.

Word was then sent to the Benjamites that 400 wives had
been procured for them. The Benjamites, responding to this
gesture of peace, came out of hiding, and 400 of them chose
wives from among the captured young women.

Apparently blaming the war and its disastrous results for Benjamin on the Lord (Jud. 21:15), the Israelites continued to
grieve over the future of the tribe of Benjamin because 200 men
still needed wives. Once again the Israelites devised a plan.
They remembered an annual feast was about to be celebrated at
Shiloh, probably the Feast of Tabernacles, since it was then
that the grape harvest was celebrated in the vineyards with
dancing and feasting.

The 200 Benjamites were instructed to hide in the vineyards.
As the dancing got underway, they were urged to rush out, seize
one of the young women, and flee with her to Benjamin. If a
father or brother of the brides complained, the Benjamites were
to explain they had the support of the elders of Israel. Furthermore, the Israelites were not to consider themselves as violating
the oath since they were not giving their daughters to the
Benjamites—their daughters were being kidnapped! Thus,
through employing a clever scheme, the people got around
their oath (Jud. 21:1), and the tribe of Benjamin was saved
from extinction.

Reflecting on Israel's actions, one writer declares:

> This is Israel, the people of God: infirm and wavering where good is to be accomplished; quick and decisive where patience and forbearance would become them; tolerant of what is only against God; fierce and unsparing in judgment save only of themselves; scrupulously keeping an insane oath yet managing to evade it by Jesuitry that deceives no one.[8]

Concluding Message of the Book of Judges (21:25)

The final verse of the Book of Judges is an editorial comment, drawing our attention again to the fact that the religious apostasy, moral collapse, and political anarchy of this period in Israel's history existed because Israel had no single theocratic ruler to uphold the Laws of God. Instead, men chose to be guided by their own desires. History once again is repeating itself. Gary Inrig states,

> We are living in the middle of a thick moral fog. Millions around us are committed to doing what is right in their own eyes. That is the path of personal and social disaster. God has called us to listen to His direction. The path to safety is the converse of Judges 21:25. Not "everyone did what was right in his own eyes," but "everyone did what was right in His eyes." When men in the time of the judges lived by that standard, God used them to bring freedom and victory to His people.[9]

Though human failure stands out in bold relief in the Book of Judges, the book is also full of many evidences of God's work among His people. In light of that truth, we must consider the following theological truths (adapted from Arthur Cundall's book, *Judges and Ruth*).[10]

● *The holiness of God.* The Book of Judges paints a grim picture of a nation forsaking the holy God in favor of pagan deities, gods of filth and uncleanness. Because such sinful actions were an affront to God's holy character, He visited His people with painful judgments generation after generation. In the Law handed down at Sinai, God had made it abundantly clear that Israel was neither to worship nor serve any other gods: "For I, the LORD your God, am a jealous God, visiting the iniquity of the fathers on the children, on the third and fourth generations of those who hate Me, but showing loving-kindness to thousands, to those who love Me and keep My commandments" (Ex. 20:5-6). Later, Solomon would affirm, "Righteousness exalts a nation, but sin is a disgrace to any people" (Prov. 14:34).

Though God is primarily dealing with individuals in this age, He continues to judge sin when it is expressed individually and collectively. A century ago Alexis, Comte de Tocqueville, said,

> I sought for the greatness and genius of America in her commodious harbors and her ample rivers, and it was not there; in her fertile lands and boundless prairies, and it was not there. Not until I went to the churches of America and heard her pulpits aflame with righteousness did I understand the secret of her genius and power. America is great because she is good, and if America ceases to be good, America will cease to be great.

Sadly, there are many evidences that America has ceased to be good. A recent issue of *Christian School Comment* stated that in 1940 the top offenses in public schools were as follows: talking, chewing gum, making noise, running in the halls, getting out of turn in line, wearing improper clothing, and not putting paper in wastebaskets.

In 1982 the top offenses were: rape, robbery, assault, burglary, arson, bombings, murder, suicide, absenteeism, vandalism, extortion, drug abuse, alcohol abuse, gang warfare, pregnancies, abortions, venereal disease.[11]

Certainly these things constitute a miniature of our entire society and are an affront to God's holy character.

● *The sovereignty of God.* If our study of the Book of Judges focused only on the chaotic nature of this period of history, we could easily assume God was not sovereign. Scripture, however, clearly reveals His sovereign power as He worked through the human deliverers He raised up and empowered with strength. Gideon, perhaps the greatest of the judges, seemed aware only of his own inability and lack of qualifications, but it was God's power and promise that was the key to the situation: "I will be with you, and you shall defeat Midian as one man" (6:16).

Abraham Lincoln in 1863 declared, "It is the duty of nations as well as of men to owe their dependence upon the overruling power of God."

Such statements need to resound in the halls of power where too often God's sovereignty is ignored.

● *The grace of God.* With relentless frequency, the cycles of rebellion, retribution, repentance, and restoration repeat themselves in the Book of Judges. We are thus quickly repulsed by the sinfulness and fickleness of the people but so easy overlook the reverse side of the coin, that is, the wonderful manifestation of the compassion and grace of God reaching out to intervene on behalf of a wayward people. Arthur Cundall says:

> His arms are stretched out still to welcome the penitent supplicant. The forbearance of God, and the wonderful possibility of a new beginning through His grace strikes a glad note in this book which cannot be silenced by the discordant sounds which appear to predominate.[12]

● *The importance of faith in God.* Though the broader strokes of the author paint a picture of gross unbelief, in the time of the Judges there are outstanding pictures of men and women who walked by faith. It is heartwarming indeed to read in the Book of Hebrews of so many judges who were included among the heroes of faith:

> And what more shall I say? For time will fail me if I tell of Gideon, Barak, Samson, Jephthah . . . who by faith conquered kingdoms, performed acts of righteousness,

obtained promises, shut the mouths of lions, quenched the power of fire, escaped the edge of the sword, from weakness were made strong, became mighty in war, put foreign armies to flight (Heb. 11:32-34).

Thus, the judges remind us that "the people who know their God will display strength and take action" (Dan. 11:32).

● *The importance of the Word of God as the basis of moral behavior.* The reason for the successes recorded in the Book of Joshua is the fact that the people and their leaders were obedient to the Book of the Law (Josh. 1:8). The reason for the failures recorded in the Book of Judges is that the people abandoned the Book of the Law, the only standard of moral behavior, and adopted a subjective standard (Jud. 21:25). It was this moral and spiritual relativism that led to the dark ages of the judges.

In our modern society few would agree the only certain basis for morality is the character of God and the Word of God. Allan Bloom contrasts the present with the past:

> My grandparents were ignorant people by our standards. But their home was spiritually rich because all things done in it found their origin in the Bible's commandments. Their simple faith and practices linked them to the great thinkers who dealt with the same material. There was a respect for real learning.[13]

Morality—what is right and wrong—is not established by popular vote. True moral behavior must be grounded on the moral absolutes of the Word of God. Few men in our generation were more convinced of this than Francis Schaeffer, who did not hesitate to express his dependence on the Scriptures and his love for them:

> It may sound melodramatic, but sometimes in the morning I reach for my Bible and just pat it. I am so thankful for it. If the God who is there had created the

earth and then remained silent, we wouldn't know who
He is, but the Bible reveals the God who is there; that
is why I love it. I don't love the Bible as a book. I love
it because of its content and who gave the content. I
feel this more strongly, emotionally, as well as intellec-
tually, each year that my life passes.[14]

It is this kind of love for God and His Word that will con-
strain us to submit ourselves to the Book of the Law, the Holy
Scriptures. We will then avoid doing what is right in our own
eyes but will seek to follow the example of Jesus Christ who
could say, "I always do the things that are pleasing to Him"
(John 8:29). Jesus also said, "If anyone loves Me, he will keep
My word" (John 14:23). Living in a society that seems to be
coming apart at the seams, we are challenged as Christians to
live courageously and consistently as people of integrity, showing by our lives that we are guided by the absolutes in the Bible
and governed by the living Lord, Jesus Christ.

NOTES

CHAPTER ONE: *Diagnosis of a National Disaster*

1. Arnold Toynbee, *The Presbyterian Journal* (February 21, 1979), p. 15.
2. Karl Menninger, *Whatever Became of Sin?* (New York: Dutton, 1973).
3. Paul Saltman, "Point of View," *The Chronicle of Higher Education* (December 8, 1982), p. 64.
4. Steven Muller, "University Professor Speaks Out," *NFD Informer* (September 1983), p. 2.
5. Yehezkel Kaufmann, *The Biblical Account of the Conquest of Palestine* (Jerusalem: Magnus Press, Hebrew University, 1953), p. 92.
6. Gary Inrig, *Hearts of Iron, Feet of Clay* (Chicago: Moody Press, 1979), p. 17.
7. Ibid., pp. 17–18.
8. Arthur Cundall, *Judges and Ruth* (Downers Grove, Ill.: InterVarsity Press, 1968), pp. 57–58.
9. Paul Enns, *Judges* (Grand Rapids: Zondervan, 1982), p. 29.
10. Cundall, *Judges and Ruth*, p. 62.
11. John E. Hunter, *Judges and a Permissive Society* (Grand Rapids: Zondervan, 1975), pp. 33–34.
12. Robert Boyd Munger, *My Heart—Christ's Home* (Downers Grove, Ill.: InterVarsity Press, 1986), p. 3.

CHAPTER TWO: *When Men Forgot God*

1. Alexander Solzhenitsyn, *Religion in Communist Dominated Areas* (New York: Research Center for Religious and Human Rights in Closed Societies, Ltd., 1983), p. 54.
2. John E. Hunter, *Judges and a Permissive Society* (Grand

Rapids: Zondervan, 1975), pp. 23–24.

3. Arthur Lewis, *Judges/Ruth* (Chicago: Moody Press, 1979), p. 26.

4. Gary Inrig, *Hearts of Iron, Feet of Clay* (Chicago: Moody Press, 1979), p. 17.

5. Henry Jacobsen, ed., "Apostasy and Its Results (Judges and Ruth)," *Adult Teacher* (Wheaton, Ill.: Scripture Press Publications, Inc., June-July-August 1972), p. 12.

6. John White, *Parents in Pain* (Downers Grove, Ill.: InterVarsity Press, 1979), p. 44.

7. Inrig, *Hearts of Iron, Feet of Clay*, pp. 26-30.

8. Irving Jensen, *Judges/Ruth* (Chicago: Moody Press, 1968), pp. 12–13.

9. Lewis, *Judges/Ruth*, p. 7.

10. Arthur Cundall, *Judges and Ruth* (Downers Grove, Ill.: InterVarsity Press, 1968), p. 70.

11. Ibid., p. 47.

12. Jacobsen, "Apostasy and Its Results (Judges and Ruth)," p. 14.

13. C.S. Lewis, *The Problem of Pain* (New York: Macmillan Publishing Co., 1962), p. 93.

CHAPTER THREE: *Three Freedom Fighters*

1. Arthur Cundall, *Judges and Ruth* (Downers Grove, Ill.: InterVarsity Press, 1968), p. 71.

2. Philipps Elliot and Jacob Myers, *The Interpreters Bible* (New York: Abingdon Press, 1952–1957), 2:705.

3. Cundall, *Judges and Ruth*, p. 75.

4. Leon Wood, *Distressing Days of the Judges* (Grand Rapids: Zondervan, 1975), pp. 172–173.

5. Gary Inrig, *Hearts of Iron, Feet of Clay* (Chicago: Moody Press, 1979), p. 5.

6. William Barclay, *The Gospel of Mark* (Philadelphia: The Westminster Press, 1975), pp. 203–205).

CHAPTER FOUR: *Deborah: Israel's Woman Liberator*

1. Gary Inrig, *Hearts of Iron, Feet of Clay* (Chicago: Moody Press, 1979), p. 58.
2. Henry Jacobsen, ed., "Apostasy and Its Results (Judges and Ruth)," *Adult Teacher* (Wheaton, Ill.: Scripture Press Publications, Inc., June-July-August 1972), p. 21.
3. John E. Hunter, *Judges and a Permissive Society* (Grand Rapids: Zondervan, 1975), p. 54.
4. Arthur E. Cundall, *Judges and Ruth* (Downers Grove, Ill.: InterVarsity Press, 1968), p. 90.
5. Walter Kaiser, *Toward Old Testament Ethics* (Grand Rapids: Zondervan, 1983), p. 276.
6. Jacobsen, "Apostasy and Its Results (Judges and Ruth)," pp. 23–24.
7. Gary Inrig, *Hearts of Iron, Feet of Clay*, p. 81.
8. Judah J. Slotki, *Joshua and Judges* (London: The Soncino Press, 1950), p. 203.

CHAPTER FIVE: *The Man Consumed with Self-Doubt*

1. William Murchison, "Actions Have Consequences," *The Dallas Morning News* (September 17, 1985), p. 10A.
2. Esther McIlveen, "Gideon—A Hesitant Hero," *His*, 37:1 (October 1976), pp. 6–7.
3. John Haggai, *Lead On!* (Waco, Texas: Word Books, 1986), p. 192.
4. Gary Inrig, *Hearts of Iron, Feet of Clay* (Chicago: Moody Press, 1979), pp. 100–101.

CHAPTER SIX: *How to Win Against Overwhelming Odds*

1. Henry Jacobsen, ed., "Apostasy and Its Results (Judges and Ruth)," *Adult Teacher* (Wheaton, Ill.: Scripture Press Publications, Inc., June-July-August 1972), p. 34.
2. Ibid., p. 34.
3. Gary Inrig, *Hearts of Iron, Feet of Clay* (Chicago: Moody

Press, 1979), p. 125.

4. Ibid., p. 131.

5. Alexander Maclaren, *Expositions of Holy Scripture,* III (London: Hodder and Stoughton, 1908), p. 249.

6. John Haggai, *Lead On!* (Waco, Texas: Word, 1986), p. 33.

7. Arthur Cundall, *Judges and Ruth* (Downers Grove, Ill.: InterVarsity Press, 1968), pp. 121–122.

8. John E. Hunter, *Judges and a Permissive Society* (Grand Rapids, Mich.: Zondervan, 1975), p. 77.

CHAPTER SEVEN: *Abimelech: The Renegade Who Lusted for Power*

1. David Jeremiah, *Before It's Too Late* (Nashville: Thomas Nelson Publishers, 1982), p. 105.

2. Henry Jacobsen, ed., "Apostasy and Its Results (Judges and Ruth)," *Adult Teacher* (Wheaton, Ill.: Scripture Press Publications, Inc., June-July-August 1972), p. 41.

3. Arthur Cundall, *Judges and Ruth* (Downers Grove, Ill.: InterVarsity Press, 1968), p. 129.

4. T. Crichton Mitchell, "Abimelech—The Bramble King," *Preachers Magazine* 58 (March-May 1983), pp. 16–19, 61.

5. Arthur Lewis, *Judges/Ruth* (Chicago: Moody Press, 1979), p. 59.

6. "Biblical Revolution Account Confirmed," *The Dallas Morning News)* (1960).

7. A. Cohen, *Joshua and Judges* (London: The Soncino Press, 1950), p. 245.

8. Carl F.H. Henry, "Reflections—Classic and Contemporary Excerpts," *The Christian Century* (November 5, 1980), p. 32.

CHAPTER EIGHT: *Jephthah: The Loser Who Became a Winner*

1. *The Rebirth of America* (Philadelphia: The Arthur S.

DeMoss Foundation, 1986), p. 151.

2. John Davis, *Conquest and Crisis* (Grand Rapids: Baker Book House, 1969), p. 120.

3. Donald Bloesch, *Crumbling Foundation* (Grand Rapids, Mich.: Zondervan, 1984), pp. 78–79.

4. Ibid., p. 79.

5. Davis, *Conquest and Crisis*, p. 121.

6. John E. Hunter, *Judges and a Permissive Society* (Grand Rapids, Mich.: Zondervan, 1975), pp. 86–87.

7. Ibid., p. 87.

8. Adam Clarke, *Clarke's Commentary*, II (New York: Hunt and Eaton), p. 148.

9. Arthur Cundall, *Judges and Ruth* (Downers Grove, Ill.: InterVarsity Press, 1968), p. 141.

10. Henry Jacobsen, ed., "Apostasy and Its Results (Judges and Ruth)," *Adult Teacher* (Wheaton, Ill.: Scripture Press Publications, Inc., June-July-August 1972), p. 51.

11. For further discussion of this controversial passage see: "Did Jephthah Really Slay His Daughter?" by Robert D. Culver in *The Evangelical Christian*, February 1959, pp. 69–70; *Conquest and Crisis*, pp. 124–128, by John J. Davis (Baker Book House); *The Distressing Days of the Judges*, pp. 287–295, by Leon Wood (Zondervan).

12. Jacobsen, "Apostasy and Its Results (Judges and Ruth)," p. 55.

13. Ibid., pp. 54–55.

14. Hunter, *Judges and a Permissive Society*, p. 95.

CHAPTER NINE: *Samson: The Judge Who Was Physically Strong and Morally Weak*

1. Robert D. Foster, *The Challenge* [a biweekly letter] (October 1, 1986).

2. Donald G. Barnhouse, "Keeping in Touch," *Revelation Magazine* (1950), p. 5.

3. Gary G. Cohen, "Samson and Hercules," *The Evangelical Quarterly*, 42:3 (July-September 1970), pp. 131–141.

4. Leon Wood, *The Distressing Days of the Judges* (Grand Rapids, Mich.: Zondervan, 1975), pp. 307–308.
5. Ibid., p. 308.
6. *Bible Knowledge—Adult Teacher* (Wheaton, Ill.: Scripture Press Publications, Inc., 1962), p. 61.
7. Gary Inrig, *Hearts of Iron, Feet of Clay* (Chicago: Moody Press, 1979), pp. 222–223.
8. Maxine Hancock, "Samson: Passion's Slave," *His* (November 1974), 35:2.

CHAPTER TEN: *Samson: Passion's Slave*

1. Maxine Hancock, "Samson: Passion's Slave," *His* (November 1974), 35:2.
2. Francis Schaeffer, *How Should We Then Live?* (Old Tappan, N.J.: Fleming H. Revel, Co., 1976), p. 205.
3. Gary Inrig, *Hearts of Iron, Feet of Clay* (Chicago: Moody Press, 1979), pp. 236–237.
4. Leon Wood, *The Distressing Days of the Judges* (Grand Rapids, Mich.: Zondervan, 1975), p. 317.
5. Lewis Sperry Chafer, *He That Is Spiritual* (Chicago: Moody Press, 1918), p. 180.
6. Ambrose, as quoted by Gary Inrig, *Hearts of Iron, Feet of Clay*, p. 244.
7. William Barrick, "Samson's Removal of Gaza's Gates," *Near East Archaeology Society Bulletin* (1976), 8:83-93.
8. Inrig, *Hearts of Iron, Feet of Clay*, p. 251.
9. John E. Hunter, *Judges and a Permissive Society* (Grand Rapids, Mich.: Zondervan, 1975), p. 102.
10. Hancock, "Samson: Passion's Slave," p. 35:3.
11. Alexander Whyte, *Bible Characters, Gideon to Absalom* (Edinburgh: Oliphants, Ltd.), pp. 42–43.
12. Alexander Mclaren, *Expositions of Holy Scripture*, Vol. 3 (London: Hodder and Stoughton, 1908), p. 254.
13. For more complete information see the following source: Ami Mazar, "A Philistine Temple at Tel Quasile," *The Biblical Archaeologist*, 36 (1973), p. 43.

14. Dietrich Bonhoeffer, *Temptation* (London: SCM Press, 1964), p. 33.

15. David Jeremiah, *Before It's Too Late* (Nashville: Thomas Nelson Publishers, 1982), p. 74.

CHAPTER ELEVEN: The Marks of Man-Made Religion

1. Allan Bloom, *The Closing of the American Mind* (New York: Simon and Schuster, 1987), p. 99.

2. William Murchisau, "The Decline of Role Models," *Dallas Morning News* (August 29, 1987).

3. Carl F.H. Henry, "The Uneasy Conscience Revisited: Current Theological, Ethical and Social Concerns," *Theology, News and Notes* (December 1987), p. 7.

4. John J. Davis, *Conquest and Crisis* (Grand Rapids, Mich.: Baker Book House, 1969), pp. 143–145.

5. John Calvin as quoted by James I. Packer in *Knowing God* (Downers Grove, Ill.: InterVarsity Press, 1973), p. 40.

6. Dale Ralph Davis, *Theological Journal* 46 (1984), pp. 156–163.

7. Ted Koppel, *Time* (June 22, 1987), p. 48.

8. Henry, "The Uneasy Conscience Revisited," p. 70.

9. Arthur Lewis, *Judges and Ruth* (Chicago: Moody Press, 1979), p. 91.

10. John E. Hunter, *Judges and a Permissive Society* (Grand Rapids, Mich.: Zondervan, 1975), p. 116.

11. John C. Pollock, *A Foreign Devil in China* (Grand Rapids, Mich.: Zondervan, 1971), p. 74.

CHAPTER TWELVE: The Fruitage of National Apostasy

1. Richard Halverson, *Perspective*, Vol. XXXVII, No. 9 (Concern Ministries, Inc.), May 1, 1985.

2. Gary Inrig, *Hearts of Iron, Feet of Clay* (Chicago: Moody Press, 1979), p. 282.

3. Ibid., p. 285.

4. William F. Buckley, "The Homosexual Stance," *Dallas*

Morning News, 1979.

5. Paul Enns, *Judges* (Grand Rapids, Mich.: Zondervan, 1982), p. 134.

6. Arthur Cundall, *Judges and Ruth* (Downers Grove, Ill.: InterVarsity Press, 1968), p. 201.

7. Samuel E. Morison and Henry Steele Commanger, *The Growth of the American Republic*, I (New York: Oxford University Press, 1942), pp. 627–630.

8. F.W. Grant, *The Numerical Bible* (New York: Loizeaux Brothers, 1894), II, 267.

9. Inrig, *Hearts of Iron, Feet of Clay*, p. 294.

10. Cundall, *Judges and Ruth*, pp. 45-47.

11. Paul A. Kiemel, "Television: A Friend of Your Family?" *Christian School Comment*, Vol. 19, No. 3.

12. Cundall, *Judges and Ruth*, p. 47.

13. Allan Bloom, *The Closing of the American Mind* (New York: Simon and Schuster, 1987), p. 60.

14. Francis Schaeffer, *Moody Monthly* (July/August 1984), p. 20.